Camino Portugués

Lisboa · Porto · Santiago

—

Maps - Mapas - Karten

John Brierley

© John Brierley 2010

ISBN 978-1-84409-181-2

British Library Cataloguing-in-Publication Data.
A catalogue record for this book is available from the British Library.

All maps © John Brierley 2010
All photographs © John Brierley 2010

Traducción española: María Pardo Vuelta, © Findhorn Press Ltd 2010
Tradução portuguesa: Ana Cruz, © Findhorn Press Ltd 2010
Deutsche Übersetzung: Sabine Weeke, © Findhorn Press Ltd 2010

Printed and bound in the European Union

Published by
CAMINO GUIDES
An imprint of Findhorn Press Ltd
305a The Park
Findhorn
Forres IV36 3TE
Scotland
Tel: +44(0)1309-690582
Fax: +44(0)131-777-2711

Email: info@findhornpress.com
www.findhornpress.com
www.caminoguides.com

Total km	Total distance for each day's stage
	Adjusted for climb (100m vertical = additional 0.5km)
850m **Alto ▲**	Contours / High point of each stage
< Ⓐ Ⓗ >	Intermediate accommodation
◀ 3.5	Precise distance between points (3.5 km = ± 1 hour walking)
─●150m > / ^ / <	Interim distances – 150 metres turn right / straight on / left

	Path or track (*brown*: earth)
	Secondary road (*green*: quiet country lane)
N-11	Main [N-] road (*red*: additional traffic and hazard)
A-1	Motorway (*blue*: conventional motorway colour)
ⓘ ⬤	Extra vigilance required / Roundabout
⬤⬤⬤⬤⬤	Main route (*yellow*: maximising pathways)
⬤⬤⬤⬤⬤	Alternative road route (*grey*: more asphalt)
⬤⬤⬤⬤⬤	Alternative scenic route (*green*: more remote / less waymarks)
⬤⬤⬤⬤⬤	Optional detour to point of interest (*turquoise*)

❓ ❎	Option or detour point / Crossroads or Junction
┼┼┼┼┼●	Railway / Station
▬ · ▬ · ▬	National boundary / Provincial boundary
〜 〜	River / Stream
⬭ ⬭	Sea or river estuary / Woodland
✝ ⸸ ✝	Church / Chapel / Wayside cross
⊤ ⸸	Windmill / Radio mast
Ⓕ 🍺 Ⓜ	Drinking font (*Fonte, Fuente*) / Café bar / Mini-market
Ⓘ 🏨	Tourist Office / Manor house
✛ ✉ ⓟ	Hospital / Post office / Petrol station
✈ ⇄ 🚌	Airport / Rail / Bus station
☀ ⁝⁝	Viewpoint / Ancient monument

Ⓐ Ⓙ	Pilgrim hostel (*Albergue*) / Youth hostel (*Juventude*)
Ⓗ Ⓟ	Hotel / Pension
Ⓒ Ⓠ	Country B&B (*Casa rural*) / Country mansion (*Quinta*)
Ⓐ Ⓗ Ⓙ	(*off* route accommodation
Ⓟ Ⓒ Ⓠ	also possibilities in firestations Ⓑ *bombeiros voluntários*)
[32]	Number of bed spaces (usually bunk beds)
Muni.	Municipal hostel
Xunta	Galician government (*Xunta*) hostel
Conv.	Convent or monastery hostel
Par.	Parroquial (church parish) hostel
Asoc.	Association hostel
Priv. (*)	Private hostel (private network with star *)

	Town plan
(Pop. – Alt. m)	Town population and altitude in metres
	City and suburbs (*grey*) with historical centre (*brown*)

Introduction: We all have too much paraphernalia in our lives – in an effort to lighten the load we have produced this slim lightweight volume of basic maps. This has been made possible by the selfless work of pilgrim organisations that have waymarked the route such that, today, we need only the barest information to get us to our destination. It would be difficult to get lost if we remain present to each moment and attentive for the yellow arrows that point the way to Santiago – mindfulness is the key. Take time to familiarise yourself with the map symbols opposite. Services along the stages from Lisbon to Porto are not yet well developed so this section is recommended for seasoned pilgrims only with a reasonable grasp of the Portuguese language.

This multilingual publication recognises the international fellowship of the camino and affords an opportunity to read these basic notes in other languages as an aid to better communication. This helps to foster a sense of camaraderie and communion – that shared intention that lies at the heart of pilgrimage. If you are not familiar with long distance walking we recommend you source a guidebook with notes on how best to prepare for an extended trip of this nature. The companion book *A Pilgrim's Guide to the Camino Portugués* provides extensive practical and historical notes (see inside back cover).

All of us travel two paths simultaneously – the outer path along which we haul our body and the inner pathway of soul. We need to be mindful of both and take time to prepare ourselves accordingly. The traditional way of the pilgrim is to travel alone, by foot, carrying all the material possessions we might need for the journey ahead. This provides the first lesson of the pilgrim – to leave behind all that is superfluous and to travel with only the barest necessities. Preparation for the inner path is similar – we need to start by letting go of psychic waste accumulated over the years such as resentments, prejudices and outmoded belief systems. With an open mind we will more readily assimilate the lessons to be found along this Path of Enquiry.

We have been asleep a long time. Despite the chaotic world around us, or perhaps because of it, something is stirring us to awaken from our collective amnesia. A sign of this awakening is the number of people drawn to walk the caminos. The hectic pace of modern life, experienced not only in our work but also our family and social lives, spins us ever outwards away from our centre. We have allowed ourselves to be thrown onto the surface of our lives – mistaking busy-ness for aliveness, but this superficial existence is inherently unsatisfying.

Pilgrimage offers us an opportunity to slow down and allow some spaciousness into our lives. In this quieter space we can reflect on the deeper significance of our lives and the reasons why we came here. The camino encourages us to ask the perennial question – who am I? And, crucially, it provides time for answers to be understood and integrated. So don't rush the camino – take the time it takes because it might just prove the pivotal turning point in your life. Whichever path you take, go well and perhaps one day we will meet at that point where all individual paths dissolve and merge into One?

J.B.

Claves para las leyendas del mapa:

Total km — Distancia total de cada etapa diaria

Adaptado para a subida (100 m en vertical equivalen a 0,5 km adicionale

950m **Alto** ▲ — Curva de nivel / punto más elevado de cada etapa

< 🅰 🅷 > — Alojamiento intermedio

◄ 3.5 — Distancia exacta entre puntos (3.5 km = ± 1 hora de camino)

→ 150m > / ^ / < — Distancias provisionales: al cabo de 150 metros girar a la derecha/
continuar recto / girar a la izquierda

Camino o sendero (*marrón*: camino de tierra)

Carretera secundaria (*verde*: carretera rural tranquila)

N-11 — Carretera principal [N-] (*rojo*: más tráfico y peligro)

A-1 — Autopista (*azul*: color habitual de las autopistas)

🛑 ⭕ — Prestar especial atención / rotonda

●●●●● — Recorrido recomendado (*amarillo*: mayoría de caminos de tierra)

●●●●● — Recorrido alternativo (*gris*: más carreteras y más tráfico)

●●●●● — Recorrido rural alternativo (*verde*: mas remoto / menos señalización)

●●●●● — Rodeo opcional para visitar un punto de interés (*turquesa*)

? X — Opción / bifurcación

++++++● — Vía de tren / estación

▬ • ▬ — Límites nacionales / límites provinciales

〜 〜 — Río / riachuelo

Estuario de mar o de río / bosque

✝ ⸸ † — Iglesia / capilla / cruz a un lado de la carretera

↑ 🕴 — Molino / repetidor de radio

🅕 ☕ 🏪 — Fuente / café bar / mini-mercado

ℹ 🏛 — Oficina de turismo / casa señorial

➕ ✉ ⛽ — Hospital / oficina de correos / gasolinera

✈ 🚂 🚌 — Aeropuerto / estación de tren / autobús

⁂ ⁑ — Monumento histórico / mirador

🅐 🅙 — Albergue de peregrinos / Albergue de juventud

🅗 🅟 — Hotel / pensión

🅒 🅠 — Casa rural / quinta

🅐 🅗 🅙 — (Alojamiento cercano pero fuera del recorrido

🅟 🅒 🅠 — también posibilidades con 🅑 bomberos voluntarios

[32] — Número de camas (normalmente literas)

Muni. — Albergue municipal

Xunta — Albergue de la Xunta de Galicia

Conv. — Albergue en un convento o monasterio

Par. — Albergue parroquial

Asoc. — Albergue de una asociación

Priv. (*) — Albergue privado (red privada con la estrella *)

Plano de ciudad y número de página

'Pop. – Alt. m) — Población y altitud en metros

Ciudad y afueras (*gris*) con centro histórico (*marrón*)

Introducción: En todas nuestras vidas hay un exceso de parafernalia. Con la pretensión de aligerar la carga, hemos creado este fino y ligero volumen de mapas básicos. Ha sido posible gracias al trabajo desinteresado de las organizaciones de peregrinos que han señalizado el recorrido de tal forma que, hoy en día, tan solo necesitamos la información más básica para conseguir llegar a nuestro destino. Resulta difícil perderse si en todo momento permanecemos atentos a las flechas amarillas: en la concentración está la clave. Los servicios a lo largo de las etapas que hay entre Lisboa y Oporto todavía no están bien desarrollados, de modo que esta sección solo se recomienda a los peregrinos curtidos que posean un conocimiento razonable de la lengua portuguesa.

Esta publicación multilingüe es un reconocimiento al compañerismo internacional del camino y proporciona la oportunidad de leer estas sencillas notas en otros idiomas, a modo de ayuda para conseguir una mejor comunicación. Esto favorece el sentimiento de camaradería y comunión: la intención compartida que yace en el corazón de la peregrinación. Si no estás acostumbrado a caminar largas distancias, te recomendamos que consultes una guía con notas sobre cómo preparar mejor un viaje largo de esta naturaleza. La guía complementaria *A Pilgrim's Guide to the Camino Portugués* (edición bilingüe inglés/español) contiene extensas notas prácticas e históricas (ver solapa interior).

Todos recorremos dos caminos simultáneamente: el camino exterior, por el que transportamos nuestro cuerpo, y el camino interior, el del alma. Debemos ser conscientes de los dos y tomarnos el tiempo para prepararnos adecuadamente. Lo tradicional es que el peregrino camine solo, a pie, cargando con todas las posesiones materiales que pueda necesitar en el viaje que tiene por delante. Esta es la primera lección del peregrino: dejar atrás todo lo superficial y viajar tan solo con lo estrictamente necesario. La preparación para el camino interior es similar: debemos comenzar por eliminar el desgaste psíquico acumulado a lo largo de los años, como los resentimientos, prejuicios y sistemas de creencias pasados de moda. Con una mente abierta estaremos más preparados para asimilar las lecciones con las que nos encontraremos a lo largo de este Camino de las Averiguaciones.

Llevamos mucho tiempo dormidos. Pese al caótico mundo que nos rodea, o tal vez a causa de él, hay algo que nos sacude para que nos despertemos de nuestra amnesia colectiva. Una señal de este despertar es el número de personas que se sienten atraídas por hacer el camino. El ritmo frenético de la vida moderna, que experimentamos no solo en el trabajo sino también en nuestra familia y vida social, hace que cada vez giremos más desviados de nuestro eje. Hemos consentido en ser arrojados a la superficie de nuestras vidas, al confundir estar ocupados con estar vivos, pero esta existencia superficial resulta intrínsecamente insatisfactoria.

Una peregrinación nos brinda la oportunidad de reducir el ritmo y nos permite dotar a nuestras vidas de una cierta amplitud. En este espacio más tranquilo se puede reflexionar acerca del significado más profundo de la vida y las razones por las que hemos venido aquí. El camino nos anima a hacernos la pregunta perenne: ¿quién soy? Y, lo que resulta crucial, nos proporciona el tiempo para poder comprender e integrar las respuestas. Así que no te apresures en recorrer el camino: tómate el tiempo que sea necesario, porque podría ser el punto de inflexión de tu vida. Sea cual sea la ruta que elijas, ve en paz y tal vez algún día nos encontremos en ese lugar en el que todos los caminos individuales se disuelven y se funden en Uno.

J. B.

Explicação das legendas dos mapas:

Total km	Distância total para cada etapa diária
	Ajustado para subida (100 m na vertical equivale a mais 0.5 km)
850m **Alto** ▲	Linha de relevo / ponto alto a cada etapa
< A H >	Acomodação média
◄ 3.5	Distância exacta entre pontos (3.5 km = ± 1 hora andar)
150m > / ^ / <	Distâncias intermédias – 150 metros virar à direita / em frente / virar à esquerda
	Caminho ou carreiro (*castanho*: significa terra)
	Estrada secundária (*verde*: significa caminho rural sossegado)
N-11	Estrada principal [N-] (*vermelho*: significa muito trânsito e perigo)
A-1	Auto-estrada (*azul*: cor convencional das auto-estradas)
0 O	Necessário muito cuidado / rotunda
● ● ● ● ●	Rota principal (*amarelo*: amplia caminhos térreos)
● ● ● ● ●	Rota alternativa (*cinzento*: mais estradas – asfalto)
● ● ● ● ●	Rota rural alternativa (*verde*: muito remoto / menos sinalização)
● ● ● ● ●	Desvio opcional para ponto de interesse (*turquesa*)

? X	Ponto de opção / cruzamento
╾╾╾╾●	Caminho-de-ferro / Estação
▬ ▪ ▬ ▪ ▬	Fronteira nacional / Fronteira de província
∼∼∼ ∼	Rio / ribeiro
⬭ ⬭	Estuário marítimo ou fluvial / área florestal
✝ ⸷ ✝	Igreja / capela / cruz à beira da estrada
⬆ ⬆	Moinho / antena de transmissão
F ⬛ ⬛	Fonte / Café-bar / mini-mercado
ⓘ ⬛	Posto de turismo / Solar
✚ ✉ ⛽	Hospital / posto dos correios / bombas de gasolina
✈ ⇄ 🚌	Aeroporto / estação caminho-de-ferro / autocarro
☼ ⁂	Mirador / Monumento histórico

A J	Pousada para peregrinos / pousada de juventude
H P	Hotel / pensão
C Q	Acomodação com pequeno-almoço / quinta
A H J	*(Acomodação perto mas fora da rota*
P C Q	*igualmente possibilidades com B bombeiros voluntários)*
[32]	Número de camas (geralmente beliches)
Muni.	Pousada municipal
Xunta	Pousada municipal galega
Conv.	Pousada de convento ou mosteiro
Par.	Pousada paroquial (da igreja)
Asoc.	Pousada duma associação
Priv. (*)	Pousada privada (entidade privada com estrela *)

▭	Plano urbanístico da cidade e número de página
(Pop. – Alt. m)	População da cidade e altitude em metros
▨	Cidade e subúrbios (cinzento) com centro histórico (castanho)

Introdução: Todos nós temos demasiados acessórios nas nossas vidas – num esforço para aliviar o peso produzimos este delgado e leve volume de mapas básicos. Isto foi possível devido ao trabalho altruísta de organizações para peregrinos que assinalaram a rota de modo a que, hoje em dia, necessitemos somente do mínimo de informações para nos levar ao nosso destino. Será difícil perdermo-nos se nos mantivermos presentes a cada momento e prestarmos atenção às setas amarelas – a solução é estarmos concentrados. Os serviços ao longo das etapas de Lisboa ao Porto ainda não estão muito desenvolvidos portanto esta secção é recomendada somente a peregrinos experientes com um conhecimento razoável da língua Portuguesa.

Esta publicação, ao englobar mais do que uma língua, reconhece a irmandade internacional do caminho e promove uma oportunidade para se ler estas notas básicas, noutras línguas, como auxílio para uma melhor comunicação. Isto ajuda a criar um sentido de camaradagem e comunhão – essa intenção comum que está na base da peregrinação. Se não está habituado a percorrer a pé grandes distâncias recomendamos que procure um guia com notas sobre como se preparar para uma viagem desta natureza. O livro complementar *A Pilgrim's Guide to the Camino Portugués* contém notas práticas e históricas extensas. (ver verso da contra-capa).

Todos nós percorremos dois caminhos simultaneamente – o caminho exterior ao longo do qual arrastamos o nosso corpo e o caminho interior da alma. Precisamos de estar conscientes de ambos e de encontrar tempo para nos prepararmos adequadamente. A maneira tradicional do peregrino é viajar sozinho, a pé, carregando todas as possessões materiais que possamos necessitar para a viagem que temos pela frente. Isto proporciona a primeira lição do peregrino – deixar para trás tudo o que é supérfluo e viajar com o que é estritamente necessário. A preparação para o caminho interior é semelhante – precisamos de começar por largar o lixo psíquico acumulado ao longo dos anos, como os ressentimentos, os preconceitos e os sistemas de crença ultrapassados. Com uma mente aberta poderemos assimilar mais facilmente as lições que se irão encontrar ao longo deste Caminho de Questionamento.

Há muito tempo que andamos adormecidos. Apesar do mundo caótico à nossa volta ou talvez por isso, algo está a compelir-nos para despertarmos da nossa amnésia colectiva. Um sinal deste despertar é o número de pessoas atraídas a percorrer os caminhos. O ritmo agitado da vida moderna, que sentimos, tanto no nosso trabalho, como na nossa vida familiar e social, atira-nos para longe do nosso centro. Deixámo-nos ser atirados para a superfície das nossas vida – confundindo ocupação com vivência, mas esta existência superficial é inerentemente insatisfatória.

A peregrinação oferece-nos uma oportunidade para abrandar e permitir alguma abertura nas nossas vidas. Dentro deste espaço mais sereno podemos reflectir no significado mais profundo das nossas vidas e nas razões porque estamos aqui. O caminho encoraja-nos a fazer a pergunta perpétua – quem sou eu? E crucialmente, dá-nos tempo para as respostas serem compreendidas e integradas. Portanto, não apresse o caminho – seja qual for o tempo que levar, porque se pode tornar o ponto essencial de mudança na sua vida. Seja qual for o caminho que seguir, vá em bem e talvez um dia nos encontremos naquele ponto onde todos os caminhos individuais se dissolvem e se fundem num Único?

J.B.

Legende:

Total km	Gesamtentfernung für jede Tagesetappe
	Für den Aufstieg angepasst (100 m hoch = zusätzlich 0.5 km)
850m Alto ▲	Höhenlinie / Höchster Punkt jeder Etappe
< A H >	Unterkunft zwischendurch
◄ 3.5	Entfernung zwischen den Punkten (3.5 km = ± 1 Stunde zu Fuß)
–● 150m > / ^ / <	Zwischenentfernungen – in 150 m rechts abbiegen / geradeaus / links abbiegen
	Weg oder Pfad (*braun:* symbolisiert Erde)
	Nebenstraße (*grün:* ruhige Landstraße)
N-11	Hauptstraße [N] (*rot:* verstärkter Verkehr größere Gefahr)
A-1	Autobahn (*blau:* herkömmliche Farbe für Autobahn)
❶ ⭕	besondere Vorsicht erforderlich / Kreisverkehr
● ● ● ● ●	Hauptroute (*gelb*: vorwiegend Wege)
● ● ● ● ●	Alternative Straßen-Route (*grau*: mehr Asphalt)
● ● ● ● ●	Alternative ländliche Route (*grün*:abgelegener/weniger Wegweisen
● ● ● ● ●	Möglicher Abstecher zu Sehenswürdigkeit oder Aussichtspunkt (*Türki*
❓ ❌	Wahlmöglichkeit oder Abstecher / Kreuzung oder Abzweigung
+++++++●	Bahn / Bahnhof
▬ ▬ ▬ ▬	Landesgrenze / Provinzgrenze
〰 〜	Fluss / Bach
⬭ ⬭	Meeresarm oder Flussmündung / Wald
♁ ♰ †	Kirche / Kapelle / Kreuz am Wegesrand
⬆ ⬆	Windmühle / Antennenmast
Ⓕ ☕ ₥	Trinkbrunnen / Café-Bar / Mini-Markt
🄸 🏨	Touristeninformation / Schloss
✚ ✉ ⛽	Krankenhaus / Post / Tankstelle
✈ 🚌 🚏	Flughafen / Bus / Bahnhof
☀ ⁂	Aussichtspunkt / Altes Denkmal
Ⓐ Ⓙ	Pilgerherberge / Jugendherberge
Ⓗ Ⓟ	Hotel / Pension
Ⓒ Ⓠ	Bett mit Frühstück (ländlich) *casa rural* / Landsitz *quinta*
Ⓐ Ⓗ Ⓙ	*(Unterkunft nahebei, doch abseits der Route*
Ⓟ Ⓒ Ⓠ	*auch Übernachtungsmöglichkeiten mit* Ⓑ*Freiwilliger Feuerweh*
[32]	Anzahl der Betten (in Pilgerherbergen gewöhnlich Etagenbetten)
Muni.	Städtische Herberge
Xunta	Staatliche Herberge Galizien
Conv.	Klosterherberge
Par.	Herberge der Kirchengemeinde
Asoc.	Herberge einer Vereinigung
Priv. (*)	Private Herberge (privates Netzwerk mit Stern *)
☐	Stadtplan und Seitenzahl
(Pop. – Alt. m)	Stadtbevölkerung und Höhe in Metern
▨	Stadt und Vororte (*grau*) mit historischem Zentrum (*braun*)

Einführung: Wir alle haben zuviel Krimskrams in unserem Leben – um die Last zu erleichtern, haben wir dieses schlanke, leichte Buch mit den grundlegenden Landkarten zusammengestellt. Ermöglicht wurde dies durch die selbstlose Arbeit von Pilgerorganisationen, die die Route dergestalt markiert haben, dass wir heute nur ein Minimum an Informationen benötigen, um an unser Ziel zu gelangen. Sofern wir in jedem Moment gegenwärtig sind und auf die gelben Pfeile achten, können wir uns nur schwer verlaufen – Achtsamkeit ist der Schlüssel. Die Unterkunfts- und Verpflegungseinrichtungen entlang der Etappen von Lissabon nach Porto sind noch nicht gut entwickelt, so dass dieser Abschnitt nur für erfahrene Pilger mit annehmbarem Verständnis der portugiesischen Sprache zu empfehlen ist.

Diese mehrsprachige Publikation würdigt die internationale Gemeinschaft des Jakobsweges und bietet die Gelegenheit, diese grundlegenden Notizen als eine Hilfe zur besseren Kommunikation auch in anderen Sprachen zu lesen. Dies fördert das Gefühl von Kameradschaft und Vereinigung – dieses von allen geteilte Ansinnen, das einer Pilgerreise zugrunde liegt. Wenn Sie mit dem Wandern größerer Entfernungen nicht vertraut sind, so empfehlen wir Ihnen, sich einen Reiseführer mit Hinweisen dazu zu besorgen, wie Sie sich am besten auf eine solche ausgedehnte Reise vorbereiten. Der begleitende Reiseführer *A Pilgrim's Guide to the Camino Portugués* bietet ausführliche praktische und geschichtliche Anmerkungen (siehe Umschlaginnenseite hinten).

Jeder von uns reist gleichzeitig auf zwei Wegen – auf dem äußeren Weg, auf dem wir unseren Körper befördern, und auf dem inneren Weg zur Seele. Wir müssen uns beider bewusst sein und uns die Zeit nehmen, uns entsprechend vorzubereiten. Als Pilger reisen wir traditionsgemäß allein, zu Fuß, und tragen alle materiellen Besitztümer, die wir für die bevorstehende Reise benötigen mögen, mit uns. Dies bringt auch die erste Lektion für den Pilger – alles Überflüssige hinter sich zu lassen und nur mit dem absolut Notwendigen zu reisen. Die Vorbereitung für den inneren Weg ist ähnlich – wir müssen zunächst über die Jahre angesammelten psychischen Abfall wie Verstimmungen, Vorurteile und überholte Glaubenssysteme ablegen. Je unvoreingenommener wir sind, desto einfacher werden wir die Lektionen entlang dieses Weges der inneren Einkehr aufnehmen.

Wir haben lange geschlafen. Trotz der chaotischen Welt um uns herum, oder vielleicht auch gerade deswegen, schüttelt uns etwas wach aus unserer kollektiven Amnesie. Ein Zeichen dieses Erwachens ist die Zahl der Menschen, die sich dazu berufen fühlen, die Jakobswege zu wandern. Das hektische Tempo des modernen Lebens, das wir nicht nur in unserer Arbeit, sondern auch in unserem Familienleben und in unseren sozialen Kontakten erfahren, wirbelt uns immer mehr nach außen, von unserem Zentrum weg. Wir haben zugelassen, dass wir an die Oberfläche unseres Lebens geworfen werden – wo wir die Geschäftigkeit mit Lebendigkeit verwechseln, doch dieses oberflächliche Dasein ist schon an sich nicht zufrieden stellend.

Eine Pilgerreise bietet uns die Gelegenheit, langsamer zu werden und etwas Weite in unser Leben hineinzulassen. In diesem stilleren Raum können wir über die tiefere Bedeutung unseres Lebens und die Gründe, warum wir hierher kamen, nachdenken. Der Jakobsweg ermutigt uns, die immer wiederkehrende Frage zu stellen – wer bin ich? Und er bietet uns die wichtige Zeit dafür, die Antworten zu verstehen und zu integrieren. Daher hetzen Sie sich nicht auf dem Jakobsweg – nehmen Sie sich die Zeit, die Sie brauchen, denn es mag sich herausstellen, dass gerade dieser Weg der entscheidende Wendepunkt in Ihrem Leben darstellt. Alles Gute, welchen Weg auch immer Sie gehen, und vielleicht werden wir uns eines Tages an dem Punkt treffen, wo sich alle unsere individuellen Wege auflösen und in dem Einen verschmelzen? *J.B.*

LISBOA – ALVERCA (Verdelha)

▬▬▬	--- ---	16.1	---	52%
▬▬▬	--- ---	4.1	---	13%
▬▬▬	--- ---	<u>10.9</u>	---	35%
Total km		**31.1 km** (19.3 ml)		

◢◣ --- --- 31.4 km (+^ 60 m = 0.3 km)

Alto ▲ High Point: Alpriarte 50 m (164 ft)

< 🅰 🅷 > *Moscavide 9.5 km (+ 800m)*

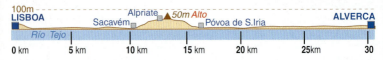

100m
LISBOA   Alpriate ▲50m *Alto*   ALVERCA
              Sacavém◻   ◻   ◻Póvoa de S.Iria
◻ Río Tejo | | | | | |
0 km   5 km   10 km   15 km   20 km   25km   30

Stage 1: Waymarks start at Lisbon Cathedral and head down to the Río Tejo at Parque das Nações and then follow the Río Trancão inland to take a tranquil valley path to the high point of today's stage at a mere 50 m. It's then a gentle descent into the busy environs of Póvoa de Santa Iria. Here we cross the railway into an industrial estate to re-cross the rail line *before* reaching Alverca do Ribatejo (no accommodation) for a short detour to Verdelha de Baixo with several pensions.

Etapa 1: Las marcas del camino comienzan en la Catedral de Lisboa y descienden hasta el río Tajo, en el Parque das Nações, para después seguir el río Trancão hacia el interior y tomar un tranquilo sendero por un valle hasta alcanzar el punto más elevado de la etapa de hoy, a tan solo 50 m de altura. Se trata de un descenso suave a los ajetreados alrededores de Póvoa de Santa Iria. Aquí hemos de cruzar la vía del tren para entrar en un polígono industrial, y volver a cruzar la vía *antes* de llegar a Alverça de Ribatejo (sin posibilidades de alojamiento). Allí nos desviaremos ligeramente hasta Verdelha de Baixo, en donde hay varias pensiones.

Etapa 1: A sinalização começa na Catedral de Lisboa e desce em direcção ao Rio Tejo, no Parque das Nações e depois segue o rio Trancão, pelo interior, acompanhando um caminho sossegado do vale até ao ponto alto da etapa de hoje, a somente 50 m de altitude. Depois é uma descida suave até aos movimentados arredores de Póvoa de Santa Iria. Aqui atravessamos o caminho-de-ferro para uma zona industrial para voltamos novamente a atravessar a via-férrea *antes* de alcançar Alverca do Ribatejo (sem acomodação) para um pequeno desvio a Verdelha de Baixo com várias pensões.

Etappe 1: Die Wegmarkierungen beginnen an der Kathedrale Lissabons und führen hinunter zum Fluss Tejo am *Parque das Nações,* folgen dann dem Fluss Trancão landeinwärts, auf einem ruhigen Talweg zum höchsten Punkt der heutigen Etappe bei nur 50 m. Dann folgt ein sanfter Abstieg in die belebte Umgebung von Povoa de Santa Iria. Hier überqueren wir die Bahnlinie in ein Industriegebiet, um sie dann erneut zu überqueren, *bevor* wir Alverça do Ribatejo erreichen (keine Unterkunft), für einen kurzen Abstecher nach Verdelha de Baixo mit mehreren Pensionen.

(Pop. 30.000 – Alt. 10m) **ALVERCA do RIBATEJO**

M *Museu do Ar*

600m Jumbo

Dormidas
☎ 219 580 475

3.8 Ponte [?]

P

P *Akí*
700m

Verdelha de Baixo 1.3

Residencial A Faia ☎ 219 574 103

N-10

A-1

3.6 Póvoa de Santa Iria

N-10

Alpriarte 5.5 *50m*

IC-2

Fábrica

500m Centro
Granja

Río Trançao

E

Sunrise

W

Sunset

S

Ponte rio 3.6 ▪ *Ruinas*

Unhos

N-10

Río Trançao

Ponte Vasco da Gama

Ponte N-10 3.8
Sacavém

A-12

Río Tejo (Tagus)

Pousada de Juventude
☎ 219 920 890
800m rua da Moscavide

2.6 Torre [?]
Vasco da Gama
Parque das Nações

MOSCAVIDE

Oriente

Pavilhão Atlántico

OLIVAIS

A-1

3.8 Túnel

Aeropuerto ✈
Turismo ☎ 218 450 657

Praça da Silva
(P. Fonseca)

Alameda do Beato

Madre de Deus M

3.1 Museu Azulejo

Santa Apolónia

Castelo S.Jorge
Iglesia Santiago

(Pop. 550.000 – Alt. catedral 55m) **LISBOA**

P

Sé ☎ 218 864 400

0.0 Sé Catedral

Turismo ☎ 210 312 700

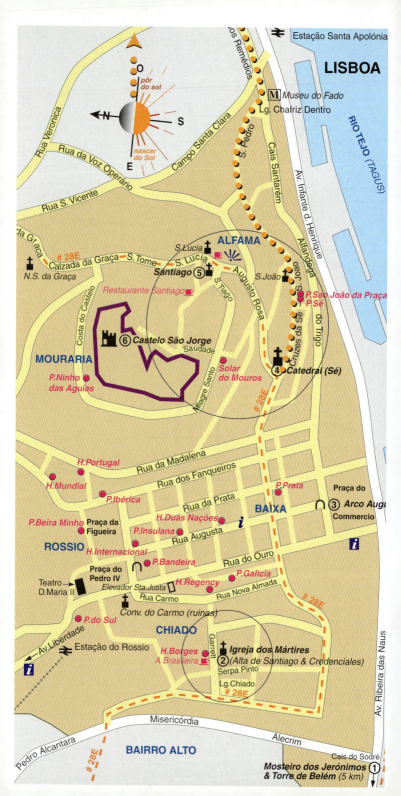

Lisbon, modern capital of Portugal, rises from the ashes of the earthquake of 1755, which destroyed the majority of the great historic buildings – the XVth century *Mosteiro dos Jerónimos* and adjacent *Torre de Belém* are outstanding examples of Manueline architecture that survived. The city has a wide range of accommodation in all price brackets – the tourist offices at the airport (+351) (218 450 657) and the city centre (210 321 700) provide full details. A pilgrim passport *credencial* is available from the Basilica of the Martyrs *Basilica dos Mártires* (213 462 465) in Rua Garrett (opposite Hotel Borges) in the fashionable Chiado district. Tram # 28E passes the XIth century cathedral *Sé* and the Church of St. James *Igreja S. Tiago* (400m above at viewpoint *miradouro* Santa Lucia); both are located in the atmospheric Alfama district below the ruins of St George's castle *castelo São Jorge*.

Lisboa, la capital moderna de Portugal, se alza sobre las cenizas del terremoto de 1755, que destruyó la mayor parte de los grandes edificios históricos. El Mosteiro dos Jerónimos, del siglo XV, y la contigua Torre de Belém, son dos importantes ejemplos de arquitectura manuelina supervivientes. La ciudad posee un amplio rango de alojamiento de todos los precios. Las oficinas de turismo del aeropuerto (+351 218 450 657) y del centro de la ciudad (210 231 700) proporcionan todo tipo de detalles acerca de ellos. Se puede conseguir una credencial del peregrino en la Basílica dos Mártires (213 462 465), en la Rua Garrett (enfrente del Hotel Borges), situada en el moderno barrio de Chiado. El tranvía # 28E pasa por la catedral (sé) del siglo XI y Igreja S. Tiago (a 400 metros de altura, en el miradouro de Santa Luzia). Las dos están situadas en el evocador barrio de Alfama, bajo las ruinas del castelo de São Jorge.

Lisboa, a moderna cidade de Portugal, ergue-se das cinzas do terramoto de 1755, o qual destruiu a maioria dos grandes edifícios históricos – o *Mosteiro dos Jerónimos* do século XV e a adjacente *Torre de Belém* são exemplos remarcáveis da arquitectura Manuelina que lhe resistiram. A cidade tem uma grande variedade de acomodações abrangendo todos os preços – os postos de turismo do aeroporto (+351) (218 450 657) e do centro da cidade (210 321 700) têm toda a informação. Pode-se obter uma *credencial* do passaporte de peregrino na Basílica dos Mártires (213 462 465) na Rua Garrett (em frente ao Hotel Borges) na zona famosa do Chiado. O eléctrico nº 28E passa pela Sé Catedral, do século XI, e pela Igreja de S. Tiago (400m acima vista panorâmica *Miradouro* de Santa Luzia); ambas as igrejas estão situadas no bairro pitoresco de Alfama no sopé das ruínas do Castelo de São Jorge.

Lissabon, Portugals moderne Hauptstadt, erhebt sich aus der Asche des Erdbebens von 1755, das die meisten der großen historischen Gebäude zerstört hat – das *Mosteiro dos Jerónimos* aus dem 15. Jahrhundert und der benachbarte *Torre de Belém* sind herausragende Beispiele manuelinischer Architektur, die überlebt haben. Die Stadt verfügt über eine große Palette an Unterkünften in allen Preisklassen – die Touristeninformationen am Flughafen (+351) (218 450 657) und im Stadtzentrum (210 321 700) liefern detaillierte Informationen hierzu. Ein Pilgerausweis – *credencial* – ist an der *Basilica dos Mártires* (213 462 465) in der Rua Garrett (gegenüber vom Hotel Borges) im modernen Chiado-Viertel erhältlich. Die Straßenbahn 28E führt an der Kathedrale *Sé* aus dem 11. Jahrhundert und an der Kirche des Heiligen Jakobus – *Igreja S. Tiago* – vorbei (400 m nach oben am Aussichtspunkt, *miradouro* Santa Lucia); beide liegen im stimmungsvollen Alfama-Viertel unterhalb der Ruinen der Burg *Castelo de São Jorge*.

ALVERCA (Verdelha) – AZAMBUJA

--- ---	1.0 --- ---	3%
--- ---	16.8 --- ---	55%
--- ---	<u>13.0</u> --- ---	42%
Total km	**30.8 km** (19.1 ml)	

--- --- 31.1 km (+^ 50 m = 0.3 km)

Alto ▲ Vila Nova da Rainha 30 m (98 ft)

< 🅰 🏠 > *Vila Franca de Xira 11.4 km*

Stage 2: A level day's walk, much of it parallel to the busy N-10 that we have to join at several stages and so the majority of our journey is on asphalt and much of it through built-up industrial areas interspersed with some quieter country lanes around the fertile river valley *Vala do Carregado.* Note the first 3 days out of Lisbon (as far as Santarém) coincide with the route to Fátima *Caminho do Tejo / Ribatejo* (blue arrows to Fátima / yellow arrows to Santiago).

Etapa 2: Un día de camino llano, una buena parte del cual discurre en paralelo a la transitada N-10, que tendremos que seguir en varios momentos. Por lo tanto, la mayor parte de nuestro día transcurrirá sobre el asfalto y durante una buena parte del mismo atravesaremos zonas industriales urbanizadas, intercaladas con callejuelas campestres mucho más tranquilas en los alrededores del fértil valle de río Vala do Carregado. Se ha de tener en cuenta que los tres primeros días fuera de Lisboa (hasta llegar a Santarém) coinciden con la ruta hacia Fátima, Caminho do Tejo/Ribatejo (las flechas azules indican el camino a Fátima y las flechas amarillas el camino a Santiago).

Etapa 2: Uma caminhada plana cuja maior parte é paralela à movimentada N-10, à qual nos temos de juntar várias vezes e por isso, a maior parte da nossa jornada é sobre asfalto e na sua maioria em grandes zonas industriais intercaladas com alguns caminhos rurais mais sossegados em redor do vale fértil do rio em *Vala do Carregado.* Note-se que os primeiros 3 dias da saída de Lisboa (até Santarém) coincidem com a rota para Fátima *Caminho do Tejo / Ribatejo* (setas azuis para Fátima / setas amarelas para Santiago).

Etappe 2: Ein Tagesmarsch zu ebener Strecke, weitgehend parallel zur viel befahrenen N10, der wir uns an verschiedenen Punkten anschließen müssen. Der größte Teil unserer Wanderung findet somit auf Asphalt statt und viel davon führt durch zugebautes Industriegebiet, durchsetzt mit einigen ruhigeren Landstraßen im Bereich des fruchtbaren Flusstals *Vala do Carregado.* Achtung: die Route der ersten drei Tage aus Lissabon heraus (bis Santarém) fällt zusammen mit der Route nach Fátima *Caminho do Tejo / Ribatejo* (blaue Pfeile nach Fátima / gelbe Pfeile nach Santiago).

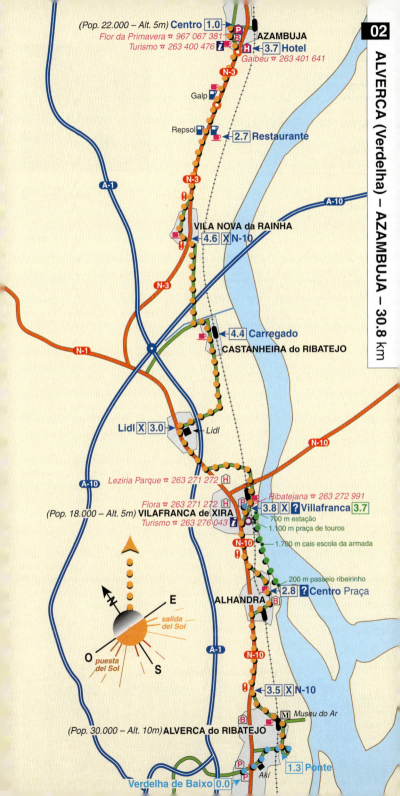

(Pop. 22.000 – Alt. 5m) Centro 1.0

AZAMBUJA

Flor da Primavera ☎ 967 067 381

Turismo ☎ 263 400 476

3.7 Hotel

Gaibéu ☎ 263 401 641

N-3

Galp

Repsol 2.7 Restaurante

N-3

N-3

VILA NOVA da RAINHA

4.6 N-10

A-10

N-3

4.4 Carregado

CASTANHEIRA do RIBATEJO

N-1

Lidl 3.0 *Lidl*

A-10

Leziria Parque ☎ 263 271 272

Ribatejana ☎ 263 272 991

Flora ☎ 263 271 272

3.8 Villafranca 3.7

(Pop. 18.000 – Alt. 5m) VILAFRANCA de XIRA

Turismo ☎ 263 276 043

N-10

700 m estação

1.100 m praça de touros

1.700 m cais escola da armada

N-10

200 m passeio ribeirinho

2.8 Centro Praça

ALHANDRA

A-1

N-10

N-10

3.5 N-10

M *Museu do Ar*

(Pop. 30.000 – Alt. 10m) ALVERCA do RIBATEJO

1.3 Ponte

Akí

Verdelha de Baixo 0.0

E

salida del Sol

O *puesta del Sol*

S

AZAMBUJA – SANTARÉM

───	--- ---	18.7	--- ---	58%
───	--- ---	13.6	--- ---	42%
───	--- ---	0.0	--- ---	0%
Total km		**32.3 km** (20.1 ml)		

⛰	--- ---	33.0 km (+^ 140 m = 0.7 km)
Alto ▲		Santarém 135 m (443 ft)

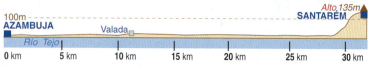

Stage 3: Today we traverse the flood plains – half the route is via farm tracks through Lisbon's 'market garden' (mostly tomatoes) and vineyards fed by the rich alluvial soil of the rio Tejo. The only climb on this stage is up to Santarém at 135m and this occurs at the end of a long day. Shade is limited to occasional stands of poplar so take precautions against the sun and bring some food and water as facilities are few and far between.

Etapa 3: Hoy cruzaremos las planicies aluviales. La mitad del recorrido transcurre por senderos campestres que atraviesan el «mercado de la huerta» de Lisboa (compuesto principalmente por tomates) y viñas alimentadas por el rico suelo aluvial del río Tajo. La única subida en esta etapa está en la llegada a Santarém, a 135 m, que tiene lugar al final de un largo día. La sombra es escasa, proporcionada tan solo por álamos esporádicos, así que protégete del sol y lleva contigo agua y comida, ya que los servicios son escasos y distantes entre ellos.

Etapa 3: Hoje atravessamos a zona das planícies fluviais – metade da rota é por carreiros através do "mercado" de Lisboa (principalmente tomates) e vinhas alimentadas pelo rico solo fluvial do Rio Tejo. A única subida nesta etapa é para Santarém a 135m e isto tem lugar ao fim de um longo dia. A sombra limita-se a alguns choupos portanto protejam-se contra o sol e levem alguma comida e água porque existem poucos serviços.

Etappe 3: Heute durchqueren wir die Flussebene – die Hälfte der Route führt über Feldwege durch Lissabons Gemüse- (hauptsächlich Tomaten) und Weinanbaugebiet auf dem nahrhaften Schwemmland des Tejos. Der einzige Anstieg dieser Etappe geht auf 135 m bis Santarém, und dieser erfolgt am Ende eines langen Tages. Schatten ist auf einzelne Pappeln begrenzt, daher sollten Sie Vorkehrungen gegen die Sonne treffen und Essen und Wasser mitbringen, denn es gibt nur wenige, weit verstreute Einkaufs- oder Rastmöglichkeiten.

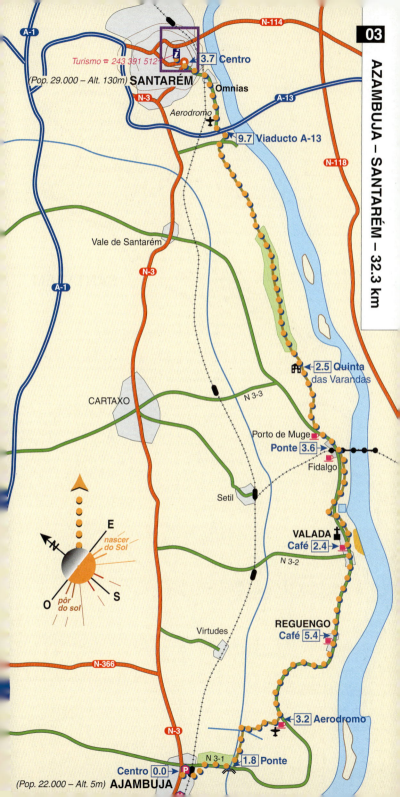

N-114

N-118

N-3

A-13

A-1

Turismo ☎ 243 391 512
i [3.7] **Centro**
(Pop. 29.000 – Alt. 130m) **SANTARÉM**

Omnias

Aerodromo

▶[9.7] **Viaducto A-13**

Vale de Santarém

N-3

A-1

N 3-3

◀[2.5] **Quinta**
das Varandas

CARTAXO

Porto de Muge
Ponte [3.6]▶
Fidalgo

Setil

VALADA
Café [2.4]◀
N 3-2

E
*nascer
do Sol*

N

O

S

*pór
do sol*

REGUENGO
Café [5.4]◀

Virtudes

N-366

▶[3.2] **Aerodromo**

N-3

N 3-1 [1.8] **Ponte**

Centro [0.0]
(Pop. 22.000 – Alt. 5m) **AJAMBUJA**

Santarém, capital of the Ribatejo, occupies an elevated site overlooking the river with wonderful views from the Gate of the Sun *Portas do Sol*. This fortified location was originally the Roman administrative centre for Lusitania under Julius Caesar and subsequently a Moorish stronghold before being recaptured by the fledgling Portuguese state under Dom Afonso Henriques in the XIIth century. The main sites of historic interest are listed (1 – 6) on the town plan opposite. The waymarked route passes the XVth century Igreja da Graça (No.4) with the tombs of Pedro Alvares Cabral (discoverer of Brazil) and Pedro de Menezes, first governor of Ceuta (Morocco). The heart of the historic town is the beautifully proportioned square *Praça Sá da Bandeira* off which is the pedestrian shopping street Rua Capela e Ivens where we find the tourist office (243 391 512) with a map of the town and a list of accommodation.

Santarém, capital del Ribatejo, esta situada en un alto, y desde sus «Portas do Sol» se tienen unas maravillosas vistas del río. Esta fortificación era en su origen el centro administrativo romano de Lusitania, bajo el mandato de Julio César, y posteriormente fue una fortaleza morisca antes de ser conquistada por el incipiente Estado portugués bajo el dominio de Dom Afonso Henriques, en el siglo XII. En el siguiente plano de la ciudad se indican los principales lugares de interés histórico (1-6). La ruta marcada pasa por la Igreja da Graça (nº 4), del siglo XV, en donde se encuentran las tumbas de Pedro Alvares Cabral (descubridor de Brasil) y Pedro de Menezes, primer gobernador de Ceuta. El corazón de la ciudad antigua es una plaza bellamente proporcionada, Praça Sá da Bandeira, de la que parte la calle comercial peatonal Rua Capela e Ivens. Allí se encuentra la oficina de turismo (243 391 512), donde hay planos de la ciudad y un listado de alojamientos.

Santarém, capital do Ribatejo, ocupa uma posição suprema sobre o rio com vistas panorâmicas maravilhosas nas *Portas do Sol*. Esta localização fortificada foi originalmente o centro administrativo Romano da Lusitânia na época de Júlio César e subsequentemente uma cidadela muçulmana até ser recapturada pelo estado Português principiante de D. Afonso Henriques no século XII. Os locais principais de interesse histórico estão indicados (1 - 6) no plano da cidade em frente. A rota assinalada passa pela Igreja da Graça do século XV (Nº4) com os túmulos de Pedro Alvares Cabral (descobridor do Brasil) e de Pedro de Menezes, primeiro governador de Ceuta (Marrocos). O coração da cidade histórica é a *Praça Sá de Bandeira,* lindamente proporcionada e donde parte a rua comercial pedestre, Rua Capelo e Ivens onde encontramos o posto de turismo (243 391 512) que tem mapa da cidade e uma lista de acomodações.

Santarém, die Hauptstadt des Ribatejo, liegt auf erhöhtem Gelände oberhalb des Flusses mit wunderbarem Ausblick vom Sonnentor, *Portas do Sol*. Unter Julius Caesar war dieser befestigte Standort ursprünglich das administrative Zentrum der Römer für Lusitanien und anschließend eine Festung der Mauren, bevor er im 17. Jahrhundert vom in den Kinderschuhen steckenden portugiesischen Staat unter Dom Afonso Henriques zurückerobert wurde. Die wichtigsten historischen Sehenswürdigkeiten (1 – 6) sind auf dem Stadtplan gegenüber aufgelistet. Die ausgeschilderte Route führt vorbei an der aus dem 15. Jahrhundert stammenden Kirche *Igreja da Graça (*No. 4) mit den Gräbern von Pedro Alvares Cabral, dem Entdecker von Brasilien, und Pedro de Menezes, dem ersten Gouverneur von Ceuta (Marokko). Das Herz der historischen Stadt ist der wunderbar proportionierte Platz *Praça Sá da Bandeira*, von dem die Fußgängereinkaufszone Rua Capela e Ivens abgeht. Dort finden wir die Touristeninformation (243 391 512) mit Stadtplan und Unterkunftsverzeichnis.

SANTARÉM – GOLEGÃ

━━━	--- ---	16.6	--- ---	53%
━━━	--- ---	14.6	--- ---	47%
━━━	--- ---	0.0	--- ---	0%
Total km		**31.2 km** (19.4 ml)	

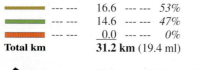 --- ---   31.3 km (+^ 20 m = 0.1 km)

Alto ▲ Santarém 135 m (443 ft)

< **A** **H** > *Azinhaga (quinta) 24.2 km.*

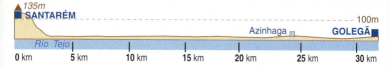

▲*135m*
■ SANTARÉM - 100m

                                             Azinhaga ▫   **GOLEGÃ**■

Rio Tejo

| 0 km | 5 km | 10 km | 15 km | 20 km | 25 km | 30 km |

Stage 4: The historic camino now leaves behind the concrete bollards and blue arrows that pointed to Fátima as we follow the more humble yellow arrows towards Santiago. This is another level day's walk along quiet country lanes and farm tracks that run parallel to the river Tejo. There is little shade and few facilities along this relatively remote section so take provisions and water and protection from the sun. Accommodation in Golegã is limited – consider booking in advance or alternatives off route.

Etapa 4: El camino histórico deja atrás los postes de cemento y las flechas azules que apuntan hacia Fátima, a medida que seguimos las más humildes flechas amarillas en dirección a Santiago. Este es otro día de terreno llano, que pasa por tranquilas carreteras rurales y senderos campestres que discurren en paralelo al Tajo. La sombra y las instalaciones son escasas en este tramo relativamente remoto, de modo que lleva provisiones, agua y protección contra el sol. En Golegã hay poco alojamiento, plantéate reservar con antelación o tomar desvíos alternativos.

Etapa 4: O caminho histórico deixa agora para trás os postes de cimento e as setas azuis que indicavam Fátima ao seguirmos as setas amarelas mais humildes em direcção a Santiago. Esta é outra caminhada plana através de carreiros e caminhos rurais sossegados paralelos ao Rio Tejo. Há pouca sombra e poucos serviços ao longo desta secção relativamente remota por isso levem provisões, água e protecção contra o sol. A acomodação na Golegã é limitada – considerem reservar com antecedência ou alternativas fora da rota.

Etappe 4: Der historische Jakobsweg lässt nun die Betonpoller und die blauen, nach Fátima weisenden Pfeile hinter sich, während wir den bescheideneren gelben Pfeilen nach Santiago folgen. Dies ist ein weiterer Tagesmarsch in ebenem Gelände entlang ruhiger Landstraßen und Feldwege, die parallel zum Fluss Tejo verlaufen. Es gibt wenig Schatten und nur wenige Einkaufs- und Verpflegungsmöglichkeiten entlang dieses relativ abgelegenen Abschnitts, nehmen Sie daher etwas zu essen, Wasser und Sonnenschutz mit. Unterkünfte in Golegã sind sehr begrenzt – Sie sollten sich überlegen, im voraus zu buchen oder nach Alternativen jenseits der Route zu suchen.

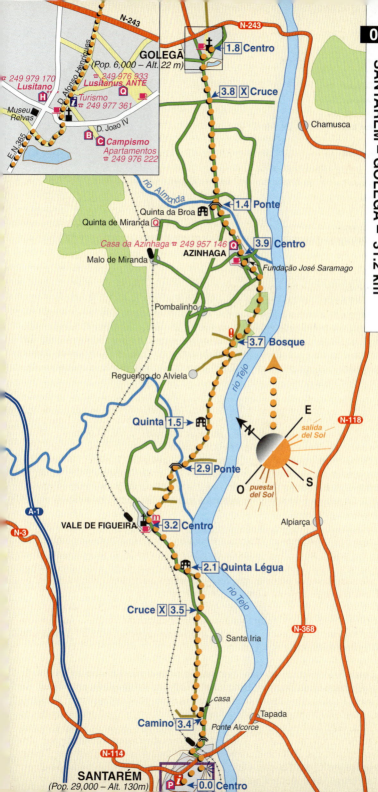

1.8 Centro

3.8 X Cruce

Chamusca

1.4 Ponte

Quinta da Broa

Quinta de Miranda

Casa da Azinhaga ☎ 249 957 146

Malo de Miranda

AZINHAGA

3.9 Centro

Fundação José Saramago

Pombalinho

3.7 Bosque

Reguengo do Alviela

N-118

Quinta **1.5**

E

salida
del Sol

2.9 Ponte

N

O

S

puesta
del Sol

Alpiarça

VALE DE FIGUEIRA m **3.2** Centro

A-1

N-3

2.1 Quinta Légua

Cruce X **3.5**

N-368

Santa Iria

casa

Tapada

Camino **3.4**

Ponte Alcorce

N-114

SANTARÉM
(Pop. 29,000 – Alt. 130m)

P i **0.0** Centro

GOLEGÃ
(Pop. 6,000 – Alt. 22 m)

249 979 170
Lusitano

249 976 933
Lusitanus ANTE

Turismo
☎ 249 977 361

H

i

Q

Museu
Relvas

D. Afonso Henriques

D. Joao IV

B

C Campismo
Apartamentos
☎ 249 976 222

E.N.365

N-243

rio Almonda

rio Tejo

GOLEGÃ – TOMAR

	--- ---	12.3	--- ---	*41%*
	--- ---	12.2	--- ---	*41%*
	--- ---	5.2	--- ---	*18%*
Total km		**29.7 km** (18.5 ml)		

▲ --- --- 31.3 km (+^ 320 m = 1.6 km)

Alto ▲ Grou 145 m (475 ft)

< **A** **H** > *V.N. da Barquinha 8.7 km (+ 500m) / Atalaia (quinta) 10.9 km*

Stage 5: We start along quiet country lanes and farm tracks as we continue parallel to the rio Tejo before branching off at Vila Nova da Barquinha. This is the point where we leave the flat alluvial plains and head into rolling hills covered in woodland providing shelter from sun or rain but requiring extra vigilance for waymarks that can become obliterated by tree felling (use the sun compass to aid orientation). We end this stage in the Templar town of Tomar, the Orders headquarters in Portugal and accordingly with strong connections to the medieval pilgrim.

Etapa 5: Comenzamos recorriendo tranquilas carreteras rurales y senderos y continuamos en paralelo al río Tajo hasta desviarnos en Vila Nova da Barquinha. En este punto dejamos las planas llanuras aluviales y nos adentramos en un terreno ondulado y cubierto de bosques que nos proporcionan cobijo del sol o la lluvia, pero exigen a su vez una atención especial a las marcas del camino, que pueden estar borradas por la caída de los árboles (oriéntate con ayuda de la brújula). Esta etapa termina en la ciudad templaria de Tomar, cuartel general de la Orden en Portugal y en consecuencia con una estrecha relación con el peregrino medieval.

Etapa 5: Começamos em carreiros e caminhos rurais sossegados continuando paralelamente ao rio Tejo antes de virarmos para Vila Nova da Barquinha. Este é o ponto onde deixamos as planícies fluviais lisas e nos dirigimos para as colinas ondulantes cobertas por áreas florestais fornecendo abrigo do sol ou chuva mas que requerem uma maior observação em relação à sinalização do caminho que pode ficar tapada por queda de árvores (usar a bússola solar para auxiliar a orientação). Terminamos esta etapa na cidade templária de Tomar, o quartel-general da Ordem em Portugal e logicamente com fortes ligações ao peregrino medieval.

Etappe 5: Wir setzen unseren Weg entlang ruhiger Landstraßen und Feldwege parallel zum Fluss Tejo fort, bis wir bei Vila Nova da Barquinha abzweigen. An diesem Punkt verlassen wir die flache Schwemmebene und gehen in Richtung der sanft geschwungenen bewaldeten Hügel, die Schutz vor Sonne oder Regen bieten. Hier ist besondere Aufmerksamkeit geboten, denn Wegmarkierungen können durch das Fällen von Bäumen verschwinden (nehmen Sie den Sonnenkompass als Orientierungshilfe). Wir beenden diese Etappe in Tomar, dem Hauptsitz des Templer-Ordens in Portugal und demzufolge eine Stadt, die ausgepräge Verbindungen zum mittelalterlichen Pilgertum besitzt.

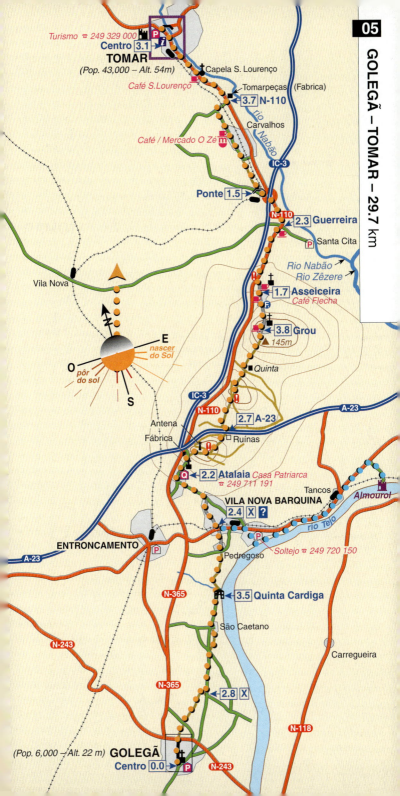

Turismo ☎ 249 329 000
Centro 3.1
TOMAR
(Pop. 43,000 – Alt. 54m)

Capela S. Lourenço
Café S.Lourenço
Tomarpeças (Fabrica)
3.7 N-110
Carvalhos

Café / Mercado O Zé m

IC-3

Ponte 1.5

N-110 2.3 **Guerreira**
Santa Cita

Rio Nabão
Rio Zêzere

1.7 **Asseiceira**
Café Flecha

3.8 **Grou**
△ 145m

■ *Quinta*

Vila Nova

E
nascer do Sol

O
pôr do sol
S

IC-3
N-110

2.7 A-23

A-23

Antena
Fábrica

□ *Ruínas*

Q 2.2 **Atalaia** *Casa Patriarca*
☎ 249 711 191

Tancos
Almourol

VILA NOVA BARQUINA
2.4 X ?

ENTRONCAMENTO P

A-23

Pedregoso
Soltejo ☎ 249 720 150

N-365

3.5 **Quinta Cardiga**

São Caetano

Carregueira

N-243

N-365

2.8 X

N-118

(Pop. 6,000 – Alt. 22 m) **GOLEGÃ**
Centro 0.0 P N-243

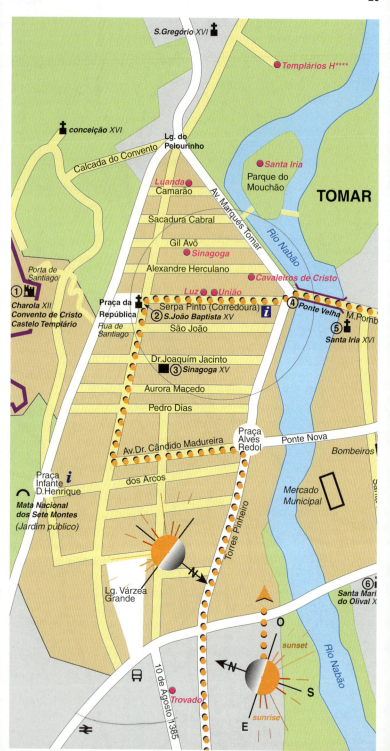

S.Gregório XVI

Templários H****

conceição XVI

Lg. do
Pelourinho

Calcada do Convento

Santa Iria

Parque do
Mouchão

TOMAR

Luanda
Camarão

Av. Marques Tomar

Rio Nabão

Sacadura Cabral

Gil Avô
Sinagoga

Alexandre Herculano

Cavaleiros de Cristo

Luz ● ●União

Porta de
Santiago

① Charola XII
Convento de Cristo
Castelo Templário

Praça da
República

Serpa Pinto (Corredoura)
② S.João Baptista XV

④ Ponte Velha
M.Pomb

Rua de
Santiago

São João

⑤
Santa Iria XVI

Dr.Joaquím Jacinto
■ ③ Sinagoga XV

Aurora Macedo

Pedro Dias

Av.Dr. Cândido Madureira

Praça
Alves
Redol

Ponte Nova

Bombeiros

dos Arcos

Praça
Infante
D.Henrique

Mata Nacional
dos Sete Montes
(Jardim público)

Mercado
Municipal

Torres Pinheiro

⑥
Santa Mari
do Olival X

Lg. Várzea
Grande

O

sunset

N

Rio Nabão

S

10 de Agosto 1385

Trovado

E

sunrise

Tomar is *the* quintessential medieval pilgrim town and the most perfect example of Templar layout and architecture to survive to this day. The main sites of historic interest are shown on the town plan opposite. The Templar castle, Convent of Christ and the incomparable *Charola* occupy a commanding location overlooking the town and have been declared a World Heritage Site. Successive Grand Masters including King Henry 'The Navigator' helped to plan the Great Discoveries from here and early navigational aids where fashioned in the town itself. Gualdim Pais, founder of Tomar and first Grand Master is buried in the Mother church on the far side of the river. Consider spending a day here to explore the Templar past and to soak up the peaceful atmosphere of this delightful town. A map and list of accommodation is available from the tourist office in the centre (249 329 000).

Tomar es la quintaesencia de la ciudad peregrina medieval y el ejemplo más perfecto del trazado y la arquitectura templaria que han sobrevivido hasta nuestros días. Los principales lugares de interés histórico se muestran en el plano. El castillo templario, el Convento de Cristo y la incomparable Charola ocupan un lugar dominante, con vistas a la ciudad, y han sido declarados Patrimonio de la Humanidad. Sucesivos Grandes Maestros, entre los que se incluye el Rey Enrique «el Navegante», ayudaron a planear los Grandes Descubrimientos desde aquí, y los primeros sistemas de ayuda a la navegación fueron diseñados en el mismo pueblo. Gualdim Pais, fundador de Tomar y primer Gran Maestro, está enterrado en la iglesia Madre, al otro lado del río. Plantéate pasar un día aquí para explorar el pasado templario y empaparte de la pacífica atmósfera de esta tranquila ciudad. En la oficina de turismo, situada en el centro, disponen de mapas y un listado de alojamientos (249 329 000).

Tomar é *a* cidade medieval primordial dos peregrinos e o exemplo mais perfeito de um esquema e arquitectura Templários que sobreviveram até aos dias de hoje. Os locais principais de interesse histórico estão indicados no plano da cidade em frente. O castelo Templário, o Convento de Cristo e a incomparável *Charola* ocupam uma posição dominante sobre a cidade tendo sido nomeados Local de Património Mundial. Sucessivos Grão-Mestres, incluindo o Infante D. Henrique "O Navegador", ajudaram a planear as Grandes Descobertas a partir daqui e os primeiros instrumentos de navegação foram elaborados na própria cidade. Gualdim Pais, o fundador de Tomar e o primeiro Grão- Mestre está sepultado na igreja Mãe do outro lado do rio. Considerem passar aqui um dia a explorar o passado Templário e a absorver a atmosfera pacífica desta cidade encantadora. Pode-se obter um mapa e lista de acomodações no posto de turismo no centro (249 329 000).

Tomar ist *die* wesentliche mittelalterliche Pilgerstadt und das perfekteste Beispiel von Grundriss und Architektur der Templer, das bis in die heutige Zeit überdauert hat. Die wichtigsten Orte von historischem Interesse sind auf dem gegenüberliegenden Stadtplan zu finden. Die Burg der Templer, das Christuskloster *Convento de Christo* und die unvergleichliche *Charola*, die Gebetskapelle, bestimmen mit ihrer Lage auf dem Hügel das Stadtbild und sind zum UNESCO-Weltkulturerbe ernannt worden. Die aufeinanderfolgenden Großmeister einschließlich Heinrich des Seefahrers halfen, von hier aus die großen Entdeckungen zu planen, und frühe Navigationshilfen wurden in der Stadt selbst hergestellt. Hugo von Payns, der Gründer von Tomar und erster Großmeister, liegt in der Mutterkirche auf der anderen Seite des Flusses begraben. Sie sollten einen Tag für Tomar einplanen, um die Vergangenheit der Templer zu erforschen und die friedliche Atmosphäre dieser herrlichen Stadt aufzusaugen. Stadtplan und Unterkunftsverzeichnis sind in der Touristeninformation im Zentrum erhältlich (249 329 000).

TOMAR – ALVAIÁZERE

--- ---	14.6	--- ---	47%
--- ---	16.7	--- ---	53%
--- ---	0.0	--- ---	0%
Total km	**31.3 km** (19.4 ml)		

--- ---	34.1 km (+^ 560 m = 2.8 km)	
Alto ▲	Alvaiázere 310 m (1,017 ft)	

Stage 6: A day of varied terrain as we climb out of the flat plains of the Ribatejo into the central province of Beira Litoral over several hills *serras* to the high point today which is Alvaiázere itself at 310m. The surface underfoot likewise changes from town pavements into dirt farm tracks, roman roads, woodland paths and quiet country lanes. Few of the tiny hamlets we pass through have facilities so stock up on water and some food before leaving Tomar. **Intermediate accommodation:** None – note there is only one *residencial* in Alvaiázere so it may be advisable to book ahead.

Etapa 6: Un día de terreno variado, ya que ascendemos desde las llanuras del Ribatejo hacia la provincia central de Beira Litoral, pasando por varias colinas (serras) hasta el punto más alto de hoy, Alvaiázere, situado a 310 m. La superficie bajo nuestros pies va cambiando igualmente, del pavimento de la ciudad a sucios senderos campestres, carreteras romanas, senderos que atraviesan bosques y tranquilas carreteras rurales. En pocas de las diminutas aldeas por las que pasaremos hay servicios, así que aprovisiónate de agua y comida antes de salir de Tomar. **Alojamiento intermedio:** No hay. Ten en cuenta que en Alvaiázere tan solo hay una residencia, así que sería aconsejable reservar con antelación.

Etapa 6: Um dia de terreno diversificado ao subirmos das planícies lisas do Ribatejo para a província central da Beira Litoral passando por várias *serras* até ao ponto mais alto de hoje que é Alvaiázere, situada a 310m. A superfície do terreno muda de pavimentos citadinos para carreiros térreos, estradas romanas, carreiros de áreas florestais e caminhos rurais sossegados. Poucas das aldeias pelas quais passamos têm serviços, por isso, abasteçam-se com água e alguma comida antes de saírem de Tomar. **Acomodação média:** Nenhuma – note-se que só há uma *residencial* em Alvaiázere e que é aconselhável reservar com antecedência.

Etappe 6: Ein Tag, an dem wir uns in abwechslungsreichem Gelände bewegen, während wir aus der flachen Ebene des Ribatejo über mehrere Hügel, *serras,* in die zentrale Provinz des Beira Litoral hinaufsteigen, bis zum heutigen höchsten Punkt, Alvaiázere selbst, auf 310 m. Die Oberfläche unter unseren Füßen wandelt sich auch von städtischen Gehwegen zu dreckigen Feldwegen, römischen Straßen, Waldpfaden und ruhigen Landstraßen. Nur wenige der kleinen Dörfer, durch die wir hindurchwandern, haben Gastbetriebe oder Geschäfte, daher sollten Sie sich vor dem Verlassen von Tomar mit Wasser und Verpflegung versorgen. **Unterkünfte zwischendurch**: Keine – es gibt nur eine *residencial* in Alvaiázere, daher kann es sinnvoll sein, im Voraus zu buchen.

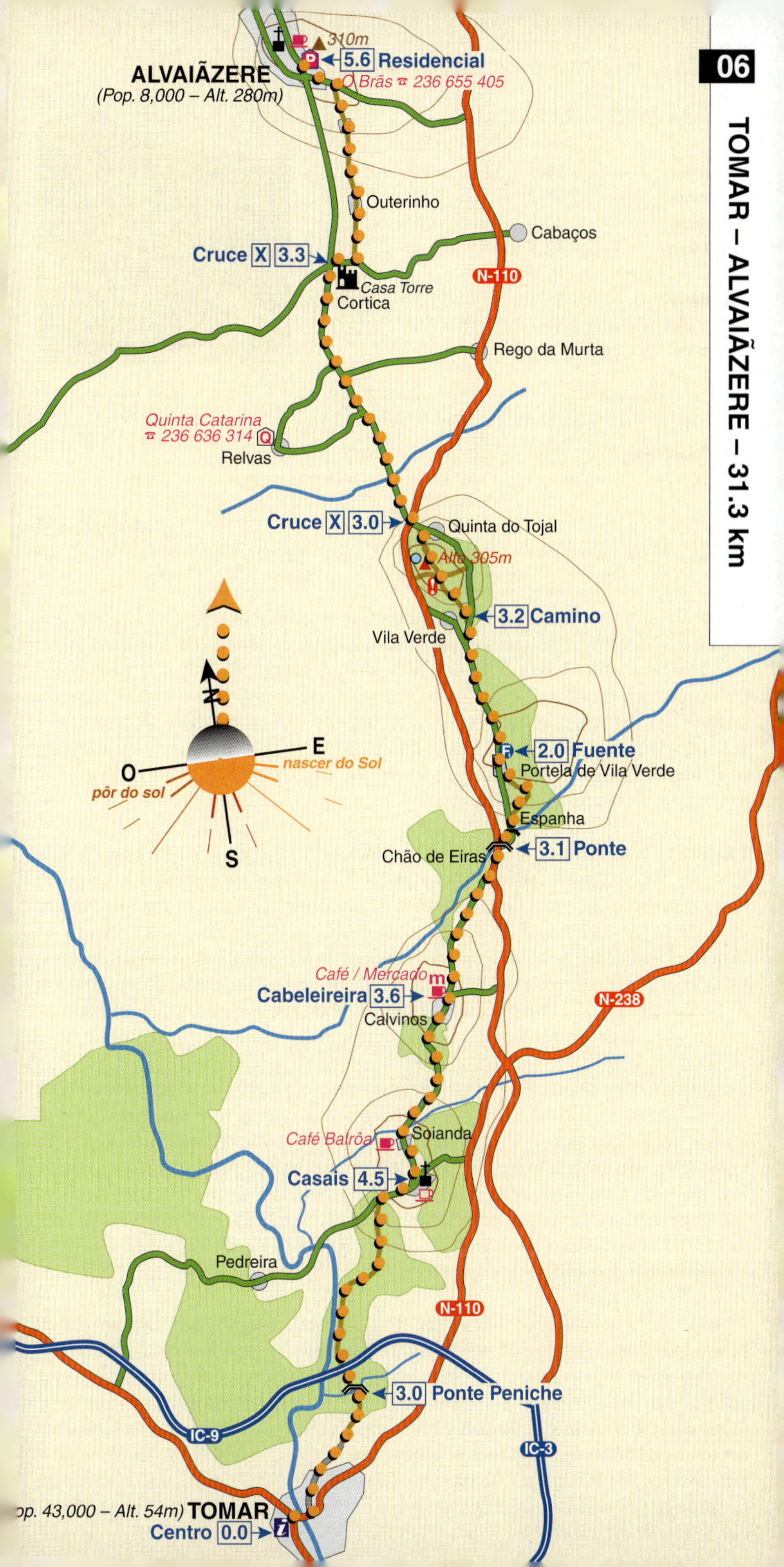

06
TOMAR – ALVAIÃZERE – 31.3 km
310m
ALVAIÃZERE
(Pop. 8,000 – Alt. 280m)
5.6 Residencial
O Brãs ☎ 236 655 405
Outerinho
Cabaços
Cruce X 3.3
Casa Torre
Cortica
N-110
Rego da Murta
Quinta Catarina
☎ 236 636 314
Relvas
Cruce X 3.0
Quinta do Tojal
Alto 305m
3.2 Camino
Vila Verde
E
nascer do Sol
O
pôr do sol
S
N
2.0 Fuente
Portela de Vila Verde
Espanha
Chão de Eiras
3.1 Ponte
Café / Mercado
Cabeleireira 3.6
Calvinos
N-238
Café Balrôa
Soianda
Casais 4.5
Pedreira
N-110
3.0 Ponte Peniche
IC-9
IC-3
op. 43,000 – Alt. 54m) TOMAR
Centro 0.0

ALVAIÁZERE – RABAÇAL

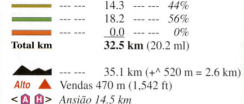

--- ---	14.3	--- ---	*44%*	
--- ---	18.2	--- ---	*56%*	
--- ---	0.0	--- ---	*0%*	
Total km	**32.5 km** (20.2 ml)			

--- ---   35.1 km (+^ 520 m = 2.6 km)

Alto ▲   Vendas 470 m (1,542 ft)

< Ⓐ Ⓗ >   *Ansião 14.5 km*

Stage 7: Another lovely day of undulating terrain through forested valleys interspersed with olive groves and small crop fields along the medieval route that brings us into Ansião conveniently located around ½ way – a good place for a midday break or possible stopover for the night. Rabaçal has recently opened a pilgrim-friendly hostel adjoining the museum (there is alternative accommodation in Panela, 4 km *off* route by taxi). The museum has artefacts of Roman origin and can arrange viewing of the Roman Villa at the far end of town, just off route on the way out.

Etapa 7: Otro encantador día de terreno ondulado a través de valles cubiertos de bosques, intercalados con olivares y pequeños campos de cultivo a lo largo de la ruta medieval que nos lleva a Ansião, cómodamente situado a medio camino: un buen lugar para hacer un descanso al mediodía o posible parada para pasar la noche. Rabaçal ha abierto recientemente un hostal orientado a los peregrinos, situado junto al museo (existe alojamiento alternativo en Panela, desviado 4 km de la ruta en taxi). El museo contiene piezas de origen romano, y la villa romana puede verse en el extremo más alejado del pueblo.

Etapa 7: Outro dia agradável de terreno sinuoso através de vales arborizados intercalados com olivais e campos cultivados ao longo da rota medieval que nos leva a Ansião, situada convenientemente a cerca de meio caminho – um bom lugar para um intervalo do meio-dia ou uma possível paragem para a noite. Rabaçal abriu recentemente uma pousada, adjacente ao museu, que também aceita peregrinos (existe acomodação alternativa em Panela, 4 km *fora* da rota de táxi). O museu tem artesanato de origem Romana e pode organizar a visita à Vila Romana do outro lado da cidade.

Etappe 7: Ein weiterer reizvoller Tag in sanft hügeligem Terrain durch bewaldete Täler, durchsetzt von Olivenhainen und kleinen Kornfeldern entlang der mittelalterlichen Route, die uns bis nach Ansião führt, das praktischerweise auf halbem Weg gelegen ist – ein guter Ort für eine Mittagspause oder eine mögliche Übernachtung. Rabaçal hat kürzlich eine pilgerfreundliche Herberge neben dem Museum eröffnet (es gibt alternative Unterkünfte in Panela, 4 km abseits der Route per Taxi). Das Museum stellt Gegenstände römischen Ursprungs aus und kann die Besichtigung der römischen Villa am anderen Ende der Stadt arrangieren.

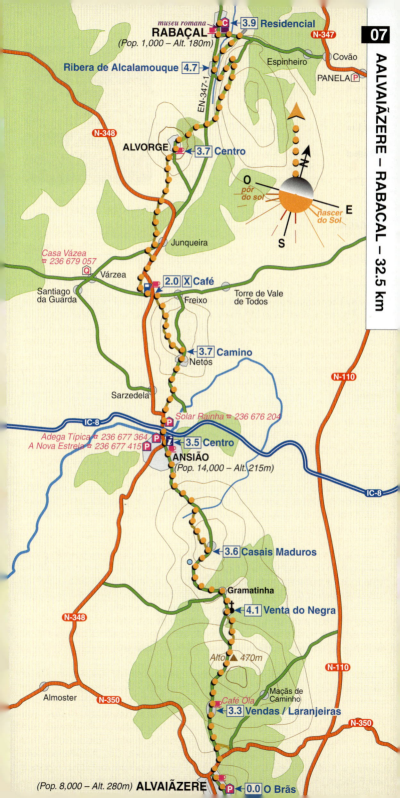

museu romana
RABAÇAL C **3.9** Residencial
(Pop. 1,000 – Alt. 180m)

N-347

Espinheiro

Covão

PANELA P

Ribera de Alcalamouque **4.7**

EN-347-1

N-348

ALVORGE **3.7** Centro

O

pôr do sol

nascer do Sol

E

S

Junqueira

Casa Vázea ☎ *236 679 057*

Várzea

Santiago da Guarda

2.0 X Café

Torre de Vale de Todos

Freixo

N-110

3.7 Camino
Netos

Sarzedela

IC-8

Solar Rainha ☎ *236 676 204*

P

Adega Típica ☎ *236 677 364*
A Nova Estrela ☎ *236 677 415* P P i **3.5** Centro

ANSIÃO
(Pop. 14,000 – Alt. 215m)

IC-8

3.6 Casais Maduros

Gramatinha

4.1 Venta do Negra

Alto ▲ *470m*

N-348

Maçãs de Caminho

N-110

Almoster **N-350**

Café Ola
3.3 Vendas / Laranjeiras

N-350

(Pop. 8,000 – Alt. 280m) **ALVAIÃZERE** P **0.0** O Brás

RABAÇAL – COIMBRA

=== ===	10.3	--- ---	*35%*
=== ===	15.6	--- ---	*53%*
=== ===	3.6	--- ---	*12%*
Total km	**29.5 km** (18.3 ml)		

--- --- 31.6 km (+^ 420 m = 2.1 km)

Alto ▲ Alto Santo Clara 215 m (705 ft)

< 🅰 🅷 > Condeixa a Nova 12.8 km (+ 900 m)

Stage 8: The terrain now becomes gentler as we leave the *serras*, our high point being Alto de Santa Clara (215m) overlooking Coimbra and the Mondego river valley. The first part follows the original Via XIX to pass the renowned Roman ruins of Conimbriga through peaceful countryside, mainly vineyards and olive groves. The latter half of the day ends less romantically as we navigate through the maze of roads and motorways around the outskirts of Coimbra. This historic university town (ancient capital of Portugal) has many links to the way of St. James.

Etapa 8: El terreno se va volviendo más suave a medida que dejamos atrás las *serras*, y el punto más alto del día será el Alto de Santa Clara (215 m), desde el que se divisan Coimbra y el valle del río Mondego. La primera parte sigue la Vía XIX original que pasa por las célebres ruinas romanas de Conimbriga, a través de un pacífico paisaje, compuesto principalmente por viñas y olivares. La segunda mitad del día termina de una manera menos romántica, navegando entre el caos de carreteras y autopistas de los alrededores de Coimbra. Esta histórica ciudad universitaria (antigua capital de Portugal) tiene una gran relación con el Camino de Santiago.

Etapa 8: O terreno torna-se mais suave ao deixarmos as *serras*, o nosso ponto alto é o Alto de Santa Clara (215 m) com vista sobre Coimbra e o vale do rio Mondego. A primeira parte segue a Via XIX original e passa pelas célebres ruínas Romanas de Conímbriga através de zonas rurais sossegadas, na sua maioria vinhas e olivais. A última metade do dia termina de modo menos romântico enquanto navegamos pelo labirinto de estradas e auto-estradas em redor da periferia de Coimbra. Esta cidade universitária histórica (antiga capital de Portugal) tem muitas ligações ao caminho de Santiago.

Etappe 8: Mit dem Verlassen der *serras* wird das Gelände nun sanfter: Unser höchster Punkt ist Alto de Santa Clara (215 m), das oberhalb von Coimbra und dem Flusstal des Mondego liegt. Der erste Teil des Weges folgt dem ursprünglichen Via XIX, vorbei an den bekannten römischen Ruinen von Conimbriga durch friedliche Landschaften, hauptsächlich Weinberge und Olivenhaine. Die zweite Hälfte des Tages endet weniger romantisch: Hier navigieren wir uns durch den Irrgarten von Straßen und Autobahnen um Coimbras Außenbezirke. Diese historische Universitätsstadt (die alte Hauptstadt von Portugal) hat viele Verbindungen zum Pilgerpfad des Heiligen Jakobus.

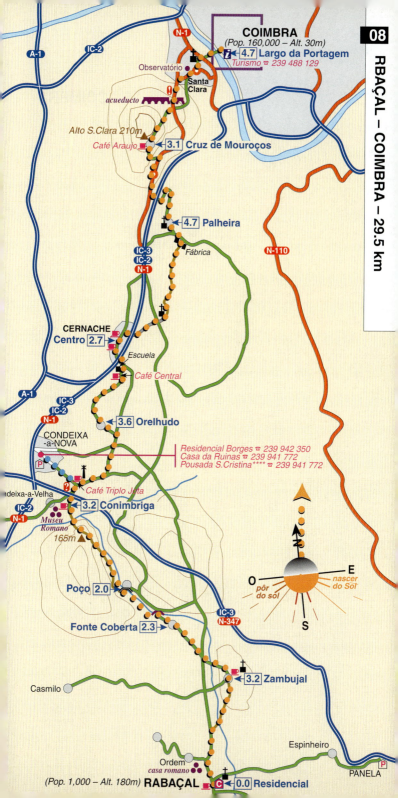

COIMBRA
(Pop. 160,000 – Alt. 30m)
4.7 Largo da Portagem
Turismo ☎ 239 488 129

Observatório

Santa Clara

acueducto

Alto S.Clara 210m

Café Araujo **3.1 Cruz de Mouroços**

4.7 Palheira

Fábrica

IC-3
IC-2
N-1

N-110

CERNACHE
Centro 2.7

Escuela

Café Central

A-1

IC-3
IC-2
N-1

3.6 Orelhudo

**CONDEIXA
-a-NOVA**

P

Residencial Borges ☎ 239 942 350
Casa da Ruinas ☎ 239 941 772
Pousada S.Cristina**** ☎ 239 941 772

Café Triplo Jota

ndeixa-a-Velha

IC-2
N-1

3.2 Conimbriga

*Museu
Romano*
165m

Poço 2.0

Fonte Coberta 2.3

IC-3
N-347

3.2 Zambujal

Casmilo

O — *pôr
do sól*
E — *nascer
do Sol*
S

Espinheiro

Ordem
casa romano
PANELA
P

(Pop. 1,000 – Alt. 180m) **RABAÇAL** **C 0.0 Residencial**

COIMBRA

Estação Velha
(Coimbra B)

Paragem de Autocarro

Rua da Sofia

João de Ruão

Castro

Carmo

Direita

N.S. da Graça

Carmo

Carmo

Inf. D. Henrique

Rua Guerra Junqueiro

Rua de Saragoça

Pátio da
Inquisição

Montarroio

Av. Fernão Magalhães

João Cabreira

Moeda

Gaia

Padeiras

Rua Olimpio Nicolau   Rui   Fernandes

Praça
8 de Maio

Câmara

Jardim
Manga

Correio

Pousada Juventude
Rua Henrique Seco 14

2 km

⑦ **Santa Cruz XII**

Santa Cruz

Martins de Carvalho

Louça

Corvo

Visconde da Luz

Corpo de Deus

Colégio Novo

Padre A. Vieira

Duarte

Madeira P.

☎ 239-828 584

Bragança H***

Oslo***

Velha

Domus P.

② **Santiago XII**

⑥ **Santa Casa de Misericórdia**
(museu da sacra arte)

Estação Nova
(Coimbra A)

Moderna P.

Poça

Praça do
Commercio

Velha

Patio do
Castilho

③ **Arco & Torre Almedina**

④ **Sé Velha XII**

O Trovador

⑤ **Sé Nova XVI**

Lg. da
Sé Nova

Internacional P.

Azeiteiras

Zé Neto

Sota

Forno

Ferreira Borges

Quebra Costas

J. A. de Aguiar

Borges

Carneiro

S. João

Astória***

Zé Manel

Fernandes Tomáz

Ilha

Atlantico P.

Largo da
Portagem

☎ 239-829 092
Larbelo P.

UNIVERSIDADE
DE COIMBRA
Velha

Praça da
Porta
Férrea

Largo
D. Dinis

ℹ Turismo ☎ 239-855 930

Avenida P.

G. Moreira

Fonte Nova

José Falcão

Ponte de Santa Clara

Avenida Emídio Navarro

Parque P.

Alegria

① *Santa Clara-a-Velha XIII*

Santa Clara-a-Nova XVII
(Urna da Rainha Santa Isabel)

Jardim P.

O

pôr
do sol

E

S

nascer
do Sol

Ibis H**

*JARDIM
BOTÂNICO*

Parque
Mondego

Estação
Coimbra
Parque

Rua do B

The waymarked route goes through the centre of **Coimbra** making it relatively easy to soak up the main sites and atmosphere of the city. Capital of Portugal from 1145 until 1255, it is better known for its prestigious university established in 1290 which crowns the hill. The main sites of historic interest are listed on the town plan opposite. The XIIth century Church of St. James (2) is directly en route but the XIIth century 'Old' Cathedral *Sé Velha* (4) is worth the steep climb up through the Arco Almedina. In this area bars and restaurants offer *fado* the mournful *saudade* music typical to Portugal. The Coimbra form differs from that of Lisbon being based more on the guitar. The tourist office (239 855 930) is conveniently located at the entrance to the town immediately over the Rio Mondego and provides a detailed map and list of the extensive accommodation.

El recorrido marcado atraviesa el centro de **Coimbra**, con lo que empaparse de los principales lugares de interés y de la atmósfera de la ciudad resulta relativamente sencillo. Capital de Portugal desde 1145 hasta 1255, es más conocida por su prestigiosa universidad, fundada en 1290, que corona la montaña. Los principales lugares de interés histórico aparecen listados en el siguiente plano de la ciudad. La Iglesia de Santiago (2), del siglo XII, está directamente en el recorrido, pero merece la pena subir la pronunciada cuesta a través del Arco Almedina para ver la «antigua» catedral Sé Velha (4), del siglo XII. En esta zona hay bares y restaurantes que ofrecen espectáculos de fado, la melancólica música de *saudade* típica de Portugal. El estilo de Coimbra se diferencia del de Lisboa en que se basa más en la guitarra. La oficina de turismo (239 855 930) está cómodamente situada a la entrada de la ciudad, exactamente encima del río Mondego, y facilita un mapa detallado y una lista de la gran cantidad de alojamiento existente.

A rota assinalada passa pelo centro de **Coimbra** facilitando a absorção do ambiente e dos locais principais da cidade. Capital de Portugal de 1145 a 1244, é mais conhecida pela sua prestigiosa universidade estabelecida em 1290 e situada no topo da colina. Os principais locais históricos de interesse estão indicados no plano da cidade em frente. A Igreja de S.Tiago, do século XII, fica directamente na rota, mas a *Sé Velha* do século XII, merece a subida íngreme pelo Arco Almedina. Nesta área há bares e restaurantes onde se ouve o *fado*, a melancólica música da *saudade* típica de Portugal. O estilo musical de Coimbra difere do de Lisboa, baseando-se mais na guitarra. O posto de turismo (239 855 930) situa-se convenientemente à entrada de Coimbra e tem um mapa pormenorizado e uma lista da extensa acomodação.

Die ausgeschilderte Route führt durch das Zentrum von **Coimbra** und erlaubt damit, auf einfache Weise die wichtigsten Sehenswürdigkeiten und die Atmosphäre der Stadt in sich aufzunehmen. Sie war von 1145 bis 1255 die Hauptstadt von Portugal, ist jedoch besser bekannt durch ihre angesehene, im Jahre 1290 gegründete Universität, die den Hügel krönt. Die wichtigsten historischen Sehenswürdigkeiten sind auf dem gegenüberliegenden Stadtplan aufgelistet. Die aus dem 12. Jahrhundert stammende Kirche des Heiligen Jakobus (2) liegt direkt auf dem Weg, doch auch die 'alte' Kathedrale *Sé Velha* (4) aus dem gleichen Jahrhundert ist den steilen Aufstieg durch den Arco Almedina wert. In diesem Viertel gibt es Bars und Restaurants, in denen *fado* – die melancholische, für Portugal typische *saudade*-Musik – gespielt wird. Coimbras Stilrichtung basiert im Gegensatz zu der von Lissabon stärker auf Gitarre. Die Touristeninformation (239 855 930) liegt praktischerweise am Stadteingang, direkt über dem Fluss Mondego und stellt einen detaillierten Stadtplan und ein Verzeichnis der umfangreichen Unterkunftsmöglichkeiten zur Verfügung.

COIMBRA – MEALHADA

━━━	--- ---	7.1 --- ---	32%
━━━	--- ---	12.2 --- ---	54%
━━━	--- ---	3.1 --- ---	14%
Total km		**22.4 km** (13.9 ml)	

◣◣◣ --- --- 23.3 km (+^ 180 m = 0.9 km)
Alto ▲ Santa Luzia 145 m (475 ft)

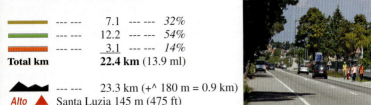

Stage 9: The terrain undulates gently as we pass along various river valleys crisscrossed with flood and irrigation channels *acequia*, reminiscent of the Ribatejo plains – the main exception being a short but sharp climb up to Cioga do Monte. While we have brief stretches of the roman road much of today is spent on asphalt and there are several dangerous stretches of main roads where extra vigilance is required. This is also a short stage so there is no necessity to leave Coimbra early. **Intermediate accommodation:** None – but several villages en route have small shops and bars for refreshment.

Etapa 9: El terreno presenta suaves ondulaciones mientras atravesamos varios valles fluviales entrecruzados por acequias, que recuerdan a las llanuras del Ribatejo. La principal excepción sería una breve pero pronunciada subida hasta Cioga do Monte. Aunque nos encontraremos con breves tramos de la carretera romana, la mayor parte del día de hoy transcurre sobre el asfalto, y hay varios tramos peligrosos en carreteras principales, en los que es necesario prestar más atención. Esta etapa también es breve, así que no hay ninguna necesidad de partir de Coimbra temprano. **Alojamiento intermedio:** no hay, pero en los pueblos que nos encontramos en el recorrido hay bares y tiendas en donde tomar un refrigerio.

Etapa 9: O terreno serpenteia suavemente enquanto passamos por vários vales de rios atravessados pelos canais de inundação e de rega chamados *acequia*, relembrando as planícies do Ribatejo – sendo a principal excepção a subida curta e brusca para Cioga do Monte. Embora tenhamos troços curtos de estrada romana, a maior parte de hoje é passada no asfalto e há vários excertos de estradas principais perigosos onde é necessário muita atenção. É também uma etapa curta e não é preciso sair de Coimbra cedo. **Acomodação média:** Nenhuma – mas várias vilas na rota têm pequenas lojas e cafés com bebidas refrescantes.

Etappe 9: Das Gelände wellt sich sanft auf unserem Weg durch verschiedene, von Flut- und Bewässerungskanälen, *acequia,* quer durchzogene Flusstäler, die an die Ribatejo-Ebene erinnern – die große Ausnahme ist ein kurzer, aber steiler Anstieg nach Cioga do Monte hinauf. Während wir kurze Strecken der römischen Straße wandern, verbringen wir heute viel Zeit auf Asphalt und es gibt mehrere gefährliche Abschnitte von Hauptstraßen, auf denen besondere Vorsicht angesagt ist. Diese Etappe ist eine kurze, so dass keine Notwendigkeit besteht, Coimbra früh zu verlassen. **Unterkünfte zwischendurch**: Keine – aber mehrere Dörfer am Wegesrand haben kleine Läden und Bars für Erfrischungen.

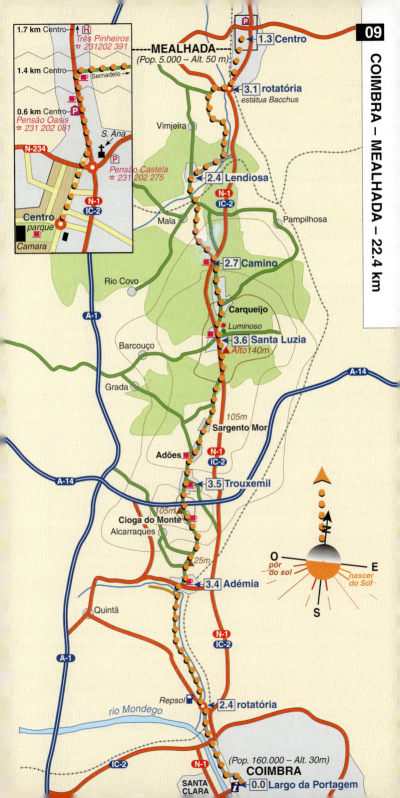

MEALHADA
(Pop. 5.000 – Alt. 50 m)

1.3 Centro

3.1 rotatória
estátua Bacchus

Vimjeira

2.4 Lendiosa

N-1
IC-2

Mala

Pampilhosa

2.7 Camino

Rio Covo

Carqueijo
Luminoso

3.6 Santa Luzia
Alto 140m

A-1

Barcouço

Grada

A-14

105m
Sargento Mor

Adões

N-1
IC-2

3.5 Trouxemil

105m
Cioga do Monte

Alcarraques

A-14

25m

3.4 Adémia

Quintã

A-1

N-1
IC-2

Repsol

2.4 rotatória

rio Mondego

(Pop. 160.000 – Alt. 30m)
COIMBRA

IC-2

N-1

0.0 Largo da Portagem

SANTA
CLARA

Inset map:

1.7 km Centro — Três Pinheiros
☎ 231 202 391

1.4 km Centro — Sernadelo

0.6 km Centro
Pensão Oasis
☎ 231 202 081

S. Ana

Pensão Castela
☎ 231 202 275

N-234

N-1
IC-2

Centro
parque
Camara

Compass rose:

O — pôr do sol

E — nascer do Sol

S

MEALHEADA – ÁGUEDA

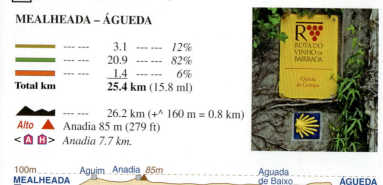

--- ---	3.1	--- ---	*12%*
--- ---	20.9	--- ---	*82%*
--- ---	1.4	--- ---	*6%*
Total km	**25.4 km** (15.8 ml)		

--- ---   26.2 km (+^ 160 m = 0.8 km)

Alto ▲ Anadia 85 m (279 ft)

< 🅰 🄷 > *Anadia 7.7 km.*

100m - - - - - Aguim - Anadia *85m* - - - - - - - - - - - - Aguada - - - - - -
MEALHEADA   de Baixo   **ÁGUEDA**
                                                                                rio Águeda
0 km   5 km   10 km   15 km   20 km   25

Stage 10: A reasonably level days walk following the path of the Cértima river valley (a tributary of the Vouga which we pass on the next stage) – the one exception being the short but steep climb around Anadia. This is another short stage but most of it is on asphalt which can be tiring underfoot. Pleasant vineyards relieve the monotony of the road network and we have the attractive riverside town of Águeda to explore on our arrival. The tourist office is conveniently located immediately over the bridge on entering town.

Etapa 10: Un camino razonablemente nivelado que sigue el valle del río Cértima (un afluente del Vouga que cruzaremos en la siguiente etapa), en el que la única excepción será la breve pero pronunciada subida en los alrededores de Anadia. Esta es otra etapa corta, pero la mayor parte de ella transcurre sobre el asfalto, lo cual puede resultar muy cansado para los pies. Unos agradables viñedos alivian la monotonía de la red de carreteras, y a nuestra llegada podremos explorar la atractiva ciudad de Águeda, situada al lado del río. La oficina de turismo está bien situada, encima del puente a la entrada de la ciudad.

Etapa 10: Uma caminhada de nível razoável seguindo a trajectória do vale do rio Cértima (um afluente do rio Vouga que passaremos na etapa seguinte) – a única excepção é a subida curta e íngreme em redor de Anadia. Esta é outra etapa curta na sua maioria feita em asfalto o que pode ser cansativo para as solas dos pés. Vinhas agradáveis atenuam a monotonia da rede rodoviária e temos a atraente cidade de Águeda, situada na margem do rio, para explorarmos à chegada. O posto de turismo está localizado convenientemente após a ponte, à entrada da cidade.

Etappe 10: Eine Wanderung auf relativ ebenem Niveau, die dem Lauf des Cértima-Flusstals folgt (ein Nebenfluss des Vouga, an dem wir auf der nächsten Etappe vorbeikommen) – die einzige Ausnahme ist der kurze, aber steile Anstieg bei Anadia. Dies ist eine weitere kurze Etappe, doch der größte Teil verläuft auf Asphalt, was ermüdend für die Füße sein kann. Ansprechende Weinberge lindern die Monotonie des Straßennetzes und bei unserer Ankunft haben wir die attraktive Stadt Águeda am Fluss zu erforschen. Die Touristeninformation ist einfach erreichbar: Sie liegt gleich jenseits der Brücke am Stadteingang.

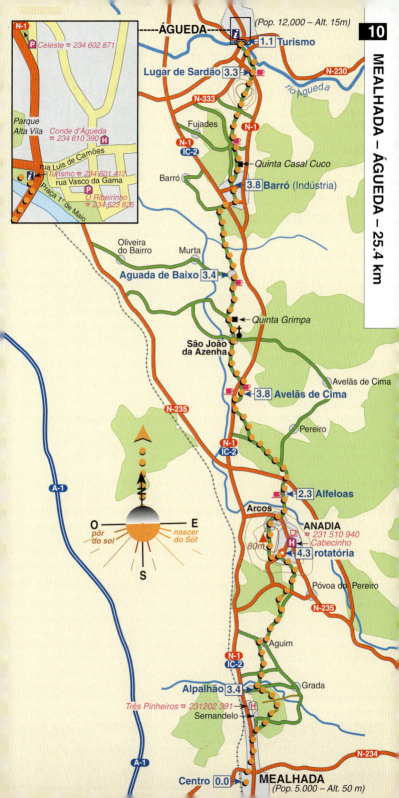

ÁGUEDA – ALBERGARIA-A-VELHA

	--- ---	3.1	--- ---	*19%*
	--- ---	13.2	--- ---	*81%*
	--- ---	0.0	--- ---	*0.0%*
Total km		**16.3 km** (10.1 ml)		

--- ---   17.9 km (+^ 320m = 1.6 km)

Alto ▲   Serém de Cima 125 m (410 ft)

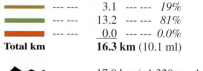

Stage 11: Another easy day's walking and the shortest stage with reasonably flat terrain, the high point being Albergaria-a-Velha itself at 130m. However the majority is on asphalt roads relieved only by a small stretch of the original Via Romana XVI over the río Marnel. While there is not much to do in Albergaria-a-Velha it is a pleasant town that provides an opportunity to just relax. Accommodation is limited – an alternative is to push on to Oliveira de Azeméis with extensive facilities a further 19.7 km (36.0 km in total).

Etapa 11: Un día más de caminata sencilla, y la etapa más breve con un terreno razonablemente llano, en el que el punto más elevado es la propia Albergaria-a-Velha, a 130 metros. Aún así, la mayor parte del camino transcurrirá sobre carreteras de asfalto, aliviado tan sólo por un corto tramo sobre la Vía romana XVI original sobre el río Marnel. Aunque en Albergaria-a-Velha no hay mucho que hacer, es una ciudad agradable que proporciona la oportunidad de relajarse. El alojamiento es limitado, una alternativa sería continuar hasta Oliveira de Azeméis, en donde hay más servicios, 19,7 km más (en total 36,0 km).

Etapa 11: Outro dia de caminhada fácil e a etapa mais curta com o terreno razoavelmente plano, Albergaria-a-Velha é o ponto mais alto a 130m. No entanto, a maior parte do percurso é feito em estradas de asfalto atenuado por um pequeno troço da Via Romana XVI original sobre o rio Marnel. Embora não haja muito que fazer em Albergaria-a-Velha, é uma cidade agradável que proporciona uma oportunidade para descontrair. A acomodação é limitada – uma alternativa é prosseguir até Oliveira de Azeméis com serviços vastos a mais 19.7km. (36.0 km no total).

Etappe 11: Ein weiterer leichter Wandertag und die kürzeste Etappe in relativ flachen Gelände, wobei der höchste Punkt bei Albergaria-a-Velha selbst auf 130 m liegt. Der größte Teil des Weges verläuft allerdings auf Asphaltstraßen, was nur durch durch eine kleine Strecke auf der ursprünglichen Via Romana XVI über den Fluss Marnel gelindert wird. Es gibt nicht viel in Albergaria-a-Velha zu tun, doch es ist eine angenehme Stadt, die Gelegenheit zum Ausruhen bietet. Unterkünfte sind begrenzt – alternativ kann man bis nach Oliveira de Azeméis weiterwandern (weitere 19.7 km; also insgesamt 36.0 km), wo es zahlreiche Unterkunftsmöglichkeiten gibt.

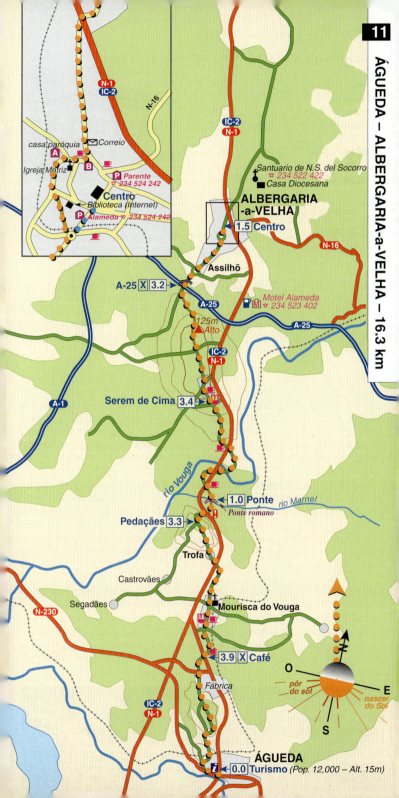

N-1 IC-2

N-16

casa paróquia
✉ *Correio*

A

Igreja Matriz **B**

P **Parente**
☎ 234 524 242

Centro
Biblioteca (Internet)

P **Alameda** ☎ 234 524 242

IC-2 N-1

Santuario de N.S. del Socorro
☎ 234 522 422
Casa Diocesana

**ALBERGARIA
-a-VELHA**

1.5 Centro

N-16

Assilhō

A-25 X 3.2

A-25

Motel Alameda
☎ 234 523 402 **M**

125m
▲ *Alto*

A-25

IC-2 N-1

Serem de Cima 3.4

rio Vouga

1.0 Ponte

rio Marnel

Ponte romano

Pedações 3.3

Trofa

Castrovães

A-1

Segadães

N-230

✝ **Mourisca do Vouga**

3.9 X Café

IC-2 N-1

Fábrica

O

*pór
do sôl*

E

*nascer
do Sol*

S

ÁGUEDA

0.0 Turismo *(Pop. 12,000 – Alt. 15m)*

ALBERGARIA-A-VELHA – SÃO JOÃO DE MADEIRA

▬▬▬	--- ---	5.2	--- ---	*18%*
▬▬▬	--- ---	20.6	--- ---	*70%*
▬▬▬	--- ---	<u>3.4</u>	--- ---	*12%*
Total km		**29.2 km** (18.1 ml)		

▲ --- --- 31.5 km (+^ 460 m = 2.3 km)

Alto ▲ Oliveira de Azeméis 220 m (721 ft)

< 🅰 🅷 > *Oliveira de Azeméis 19.8 km*

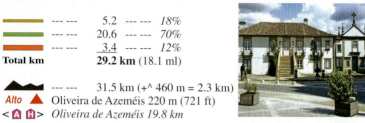

Stage 12: We start today with a stretch along a lovely forest road through mature eucalyptus and pinewoods but the route becomes progressively more urbanized as we approach São João da Madeira and have to cross the main road and railway line a number of times. The terrain is now more irregular as we pass through several low hill areas that divide 3 main river valleys. The high point today is up to São João da Madeira (220m) at the end of this stage.

Etapa 12: Hoy comenzamos con un tramo sobre una encantadora carretera forestal, pasando entre maduros eucaliptos y pinos, pero el recorrido se vuelve progresivamente más urbanizado a medida que nos aproximamos a São João da Madeira y hemos de cruzar la carretera principal y la vía del tren unas cuantas veces. El terreno se vuelve más irregular a medida que pasamos por varias zonas de colinas bajas que se hunden en tres valles de río principales. El punto más alto del día está en São João da Madeira (220 m), al final de esta etapa.

Etapa 12: Hoje começamos com um percurso ao longo duma atraente estrada florestal com eucaliptais e pinhais mas a rota torna-se progressivamente mais urbanizada ao aproximarmo-nos de S. João da Madeira e temos de atravessar a estrada principal e o caminho-de-ferro algumas vezes. O terreno é agora mais irregular ao passarmos por várias áreas de colinas baixas que descem para 3 vales de rios. O ponto alto de hoje é na zona Oliveira de Azeméis / São João da Madeira (220m) no fim desta etapa.

Etappe 12: Heute beginnen wir mit einer Strecke entlang einer reizvollen Waldstraße durch alte Eukalyptus- und Nadelhölzer, doch der Weg wird zunehmend städtischer, wenn wir uns São João da Madeira nähern, und wir müssen mehrfach die Hauptstraße und Bahngleise überqueren. Das Gelände ist nun ungleichmäßiger: Wir wandern durch ein Gebiet mit mehreren kleinen Hügeln, die drei große Flusstäler unterteilen. Der höchste Punkt ist heute bei São João da Madeira (220 m) am Ende dieser Etappe.

---**SÃO JOÃO**---
da MADEIRA
(Pop. 21,000 Alt. 240m)

[P] [3.0] Centre

Centro
Praça Luís Ribeiro
11 Outubro
Solar São João
256 202 540
Oliveira Junior
St. Antonio
Dr.Macie
João A.S.
6 836 100
Renato
Liberdade
Praça 25
de Abril
V. João Madeira
João de Deus
Igreja
Largo
Souto
Antonio M. Pinho
Araujo

Faria de Cima

[3.1] [X] Caminho de ferro

Quinta

N-227

Vila de Cucujães

São Roque

Mangas

Ponte [3.3]
rio UI

Santiago da Riba–UI

Figueiredo

IC-2
N-1

230m

---**OLIVEIRA de AZEMÉIS**---
(Pop. 12,000 – Alt. 220m)

[H] [3.7] Centro

25 de Abril
A.Pinto de
Largo S.
Miguel
i
Bento Cerqueira
Praça José
da Costa
La Salette
256 674 890
[P]
Largo da
República
Centro [H]
Dighton
256 682 191
Av. Dr.A dos Reis
Dr.M Arriaga
Almeida
Taxi
Anacleto
256 682 541

UI
105m
Ponte medieval

Travanca
Ponte [3.6]
N-224

Caniços
fonte
Bemposta
210m
passarela

Pinheiro
da Bemposta

[5.4] [X] café

Alviães
Cruce

O
pôr
do sol
E
nascer
do Sol
S

A-1

Cristelo

Escusa

Casaldima

Branca
XVII S.da Alegria

ALBERGARIA-a-NOVA

[3.7] Centro

Carvalhal

IC-2
N-1

Santuario de N.S. del Socorro
Casa Diocesana
234 522 422

[3.4] [X] estátua

A-1

A-25

N-16

Centro [0.0]
[P]
ALBERGARIA-a-Velha

SÃO JOÃO DA MADEIRA – PORTO

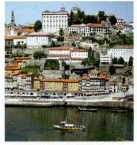

--- ---	2.8	--- ---	8%
--- ---	20.6	--- ---	60%
--- ---	<u>10.9</u>	--- ---	32%
Total km	**34.3 km** (21.3 ml)		

◣◣ --- ---	36.8 km (+^ 505 m = 2.5 km)	
Alto ▲	Malaposta 315 m (1,033 ft)	
< Ⓐ Ⓗ >	*Grijó 19.0 km (+ 1.5 km)*	

Stage 13: As we approach Porto the road network becomes more congested so prepare for the long slog into the city relieved only by a short stretch of delightful medieval road through woodland beyond Grijó. This is a *very* long stage, much of it on roads across undulating terrain, so you will need to leave São João at first light. The medieval monastery at Grijó offers some respite around halfway and accommodation is also possible here 1½ km *off* route (see map). Consider taking a rest day in Porto to recover from your exertions and to explore the city.

Etapa 13: A medida que nos acercamos a Oporto la red de carreteras está más congestionada, así que prepárate para la larga y ardua entrada en la ciudad, aliviada tan solo por un breve tramo de maravillosa carretera medieval que atraviesa un bosque, después de Grijó. Esta es una etapa muy larga, con mucha carretera y terreno ondulado, así que tendrás que salir de São João con las primeras luces. El monasterio medieval de Grijó proporciona un respiro a medio camino, y también es posible encontrar alojamiento aquí, desviándose 1½ km del recorrido (ver mapa). Plantéate tomarte un día de descanso en Oporto para recuperarte del esfuerzo y explorar la ciudad.

Etapa 13: Ao aproximarmo-nos do Porto a rede rodoviária torna-se mais congestionada, por isso preparem-se para uma caminhada fatigante até à cidade, atenuada somente por um troço curto e agradável de estrada medieval por área florestal depois de Grijó. Esta etapa é *muito* longa com muitas estradas e terreno sinuoso por isso é necessário sair de São João ao amanhecer. O mosteiro medieval de Grijó oferece uma pausa a meio caminho e também é possível acomodação aqui 1½ km *fora* da rota (ver mapa). Considerem a possibilidade de descansar um dia no Porto para recuperar do esforço e explorar a cidade.

Etappe 13: Je weiter wir uns Porto nähern, desto verkehrsreicher wird das Straßennetz: Bereiten Sie sich also auf den langen, harten Kampf in die Stadt vor, der nur durch eine kurze Strecke auf einer wundervollen mittelalterlichen Straße durch ein Waldgebiet jenseits von Grijó gemildert wird. Dies ist eine *sehr* lange Etappe, die weitgehend über Straßen durch sich sanft wellende Landschaft führt; Sie werden also beim ersten Tageslicht von São João aufbrechen müssen. Das mittelalterliche Kloster in Grijó auf halber Strecke bietet eine Atempause und Unterkunft ist hier ebenfalls 1.5 km jenseits der Route möglich (siehe Karte). Vielleicht planen Sie einen Tag Pause in Porto ein, um sich von den Anstrengungen zu erholen und die Stadt zu besichtigen.

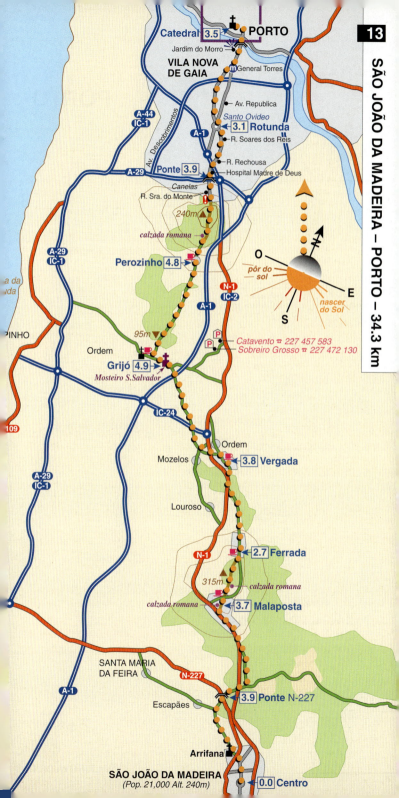

Catedral **3.5** **PORTO**

Jardim do Morro

VILA NOVA DE GAIA

General Torres

Av. Republica

Santo Ovideo **3.1** **Rotunda**

R. Soares dos Reis

R. Rechousa

Ponte **3.9**

Hospital Madre de Deus

Canelas

R. Sra. do Monte

240m

calzada romana

Perozinho **4.8**

95m

Ordem

Grijó **4.9**

Mosteiro S.Salvador

pôr do sol

nascer do Sol

O

E

S

Catavento ☏ 227 457 583
Sobreiro Grosso ☏ 227 472 130

IC-24

Ordem

Mozelos **3.8** **Vergada**

Louroso

2.7 **Ferrada**

315m

calzada romana

calzada romana **3.7** **Malaposta**

SANTA MARIA DA FEIRA

Escapães

3.9 **Ponte** N-227

Arrifana

SÃO JOÃO DA MADEIRA
(Pop. 21,000 Alt. 240m) **0.0** **Centro**

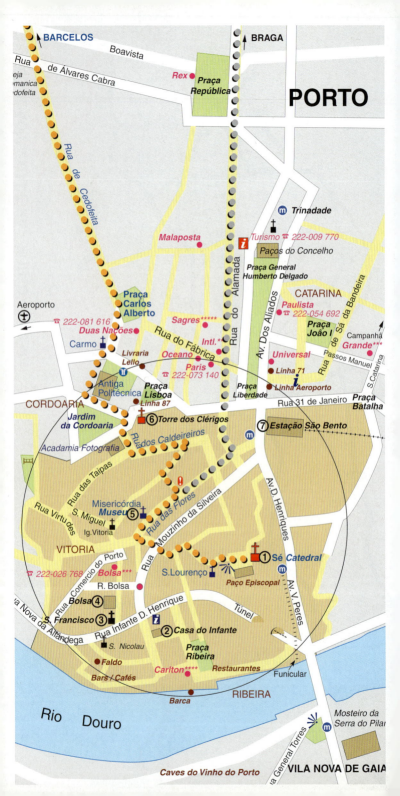

Portugal derives its name from **Porto** the *portus* that straddles the 'river of gold' *Rio Douro*. Henry the Navigator *Dom Henrique* launched the first great European voyages of exploration from here and was born in Porto 1394. The historical centre was declared a World Heritage site in 1996 and in 2001 Porto was chosen as European City of Culture. Best known for the fortified port wines that make their way to all parts of the world from the wine lodges that line the river in Vila Nova da Gaia. All this grew out of an ancient Celtic settlement atop what is now Cathedral Hillock *Colina da Sé*, a rocky promontory from which the atmospheric old quarter tumbles down to the river at *Cais da Ribeira*. A pilgrim passport *credencial* is available from the cathedral information desk. The main sites are listed (1 – 7) on the town plan opposite.

El nombre de Portugal procede de **Porto**, el *portus* que cabalga sobre el «río de oro», río *Douro*. Enrique el Navegante, Dom Henrique, nacido en Oporto en 1394, partió de aquí para realizar los primeros grandes viajes exploradores europeos. El centro histórico fue declarado Patrimonio de la Humanidad en 1996 y en 2001 Oporto fue elegida Ciudad Europea de la Cultura. Más conocida por los vinos fortificados de Oporto, que llegan a todo el mundo desde las bodegas que bordean el río en Vila Nova de Gaia. Todo surge de un antiguo asentamiento celta, sobre el cual se halla actualmente el montículo de la catedral, Colina da Sé, un promontorio rocoso desde el que el evocador casco antiguo desciende hasta el río en Cais da Ribeira. Se puede conseguir la credencial de peregrino en el mostrador de información de la catedral. Los principales lugares de interés están indicados (1-7) en el siguiente plano de la ciudad.

O nome de Portugal deriva de **Porto**, o *portus* que atravessa o rio Douro. Foi aqui que o *Infante D. Henrique*, o Navegador, nascido no Porto em 1394, iniciou as primeiras grandes viagens europeias de exploração. O centro histórico foi declarado um Local de Património Mundial em 1996 e em 2001, o Porto foi escolhido como a Capital Europeia da Cultura. Conhecido principalmente pelos seus vinhos do porto fortificados que chegam a todas as partes do mundo provenientes das caves alinhadas pela margem do rio em Vila Nova de Gaia. Tudo isto começou com um agrupamento Céltico antigo situado no topo que é agora a Colina da Sé, um promontório rochoso pelo qual desce o pitoresco bairro antigo até ao *Cais da Ribeira*. Pode-se obter uma *credencial* do passaporte de peregrino no balcão de informação da catedral. Os locais principais estão indicados (1 – 7) no plano da cidade em frente.

Portugals Name leitet sich ab von **Porto** – *portus* –, dem Hafen, der an der Mündung des Rio Douro, 'Fluss des Goldes', liegt. Heinrich der Seefahrer, Dom Henrique, der 1394 in Porto geboren wurde, startete die ersten großen europäischen Forschungsreisen von hier. Das historische Zentrum wurde 1996 zum Weltkulturerbe erklärt und 2001 wurde Porto zur Europäischen Kulturhauptstadt erwählt. Die Stadt ist am besten für die alkohol-verstärkten Portweine bekannt, die ihren Weg von den Weinkellereien entlang des Flusses in Vila Nova da Gaia in die ganze Welt finden. All dies erwuchs aus einer alten keltischen Ansiedlung auf dem Hügel, der inzwischen Kathedralen-Hügel – *Colina da Sé* – genannt wird, ein felsiges Kap, von dem aus die stimmungsvollen alten Viertel bis zum Fluss am *Cais da Ribeira* hinunterpurzeln. Ein Pilgerausweis, *credencial,* ist am Informationstisch der Kathedrale erhältlich. Die Hauptsehenswürdigkeiten (1 – 7) sind auf dem Stadtplan auf der nächsten Seite aufgelistet.

PORTO – VILARINHO
(VILA DO CONDE / RATES)

▬▬	--- ---	0.0	--- ---	0%	
▬▬	--- ---	15.6	--- ---	60%	
▬▬	--- ---	10.3	--- ---	40%	
Total km		**25.9 km** (16.1 ml)			

▲▄ --- --- 27.0 km (+^ 220 m = 1.1 km)

Alto ▲ Igreja Maia 125 m (410 ft)

< Ⓐ Ⓗ > Maia 12.9 / Padrao Moreira 14.6

Stage 14: [A] The waymarked route starts at the cathedral. To avoid the busy city streets there are several options (see map). **[B]** Start at *Matosinhos* harbour (Metro or bus to Mercado) and walk the delightful coast to Vila do Conde (not waymarked, just head due North with the sea as guide), then reconnect with the main route in Arcos or Rates. **[C]** Take the metro to Fórum Maia and join the route at Igreja Maia (0.7 km). **[D]** Take the metro to Vilar do Pinheiro and connect at Mosteiró (1.2 km) – from the latter 2 it easy to reach the popular pilgrim hostel in Rates (see next stage).

Etapa 14: [A] El recorrido marcado comienza en la catedral. Existen diversas opciones para evitar las concurridas calles (ver mapa). **[B]** Comienza en el puerto de Matosinhos (metro o autobús hasta Mercado) y recorre a pie la maravillosa costa hasta Vila do Conde (el camino no está marcado, sencillamente ve hacia el norte tomando el mar como referencia), que vuelve a unirse a la ruta principal en Arcos o en Rates. **[C]** Toma el metro hasta Fórum Maia y enlaza con la ruta en Igreja Maia (0,7 km). **[D]** Toma el metro hasta Vilar do Pinheiro y enlaza en Mosteiró (1,2 km). Desde las dos últimas resulta sencillo llegar al popular albergue de peregrinos de Rates (ver siguiente etapa).

Etapa 14: [A] A rota assinalada começa na catedral. Para evitar as ruas movimentadas há várias opções (ver mapa). **[B]** Comece no porto de Matosinhos (Metro ou autocarro para Mercado) e caminhe pela agradável costa até Vila do Conde (não assinalado, seguir para Norte usado o mar como orientação) regresse à rota principal em Arcos ou Rates. **[C]** Apanhe o metro para Fórum Maia e junte-se à rota na Igreja Maia (0.7km). **[D]** Apanhe o metro para Vilar do Pinheiro e volte à rota em Mosteiró (1.2km) – a partir dos 2 últimos pontos é fácil alcançar a popular pousada dos peregrinos em Rates (ver etapa seguinte).

Etappe 14: **[A]** Die ausgeschilderte Route beginnt an der Kathedrale. Es gibt verschiedene Möglichkeiten, die belebten Straßen der Stadt zu vermeiden (siehe Karte). **[B]** Starten Sie am Matoshinos-Hafen (Metro/Stadtbahn oder Bus nach Mercado) und wandern Sie die reizvolle Küste entlang nach Vila do Conde (nicht ausgeschildert, mit dem Meer als Anhaltspunkt einfach gen Norden wandern). Nehmen Sie die Hauptroute in Arcos oder Rates wieder auf. **[C]** Nehmen Sie die Metro nach Fórum Maia und schließen Sie sich der Route in Igreja Maia (0.7 km) an. **[D]** Nehmen Sie die Metro nach Vilar do Pinheiro und nehmen Sie den Weg in Mosteiró (1.2 km) auf – von den letzten beiden Orten aus ist es einfach, die beliebte Pilgerherberge in Rates zu erreichen (siehe nächste Etappe).

Turismo ☎ 252 248 473
[Total 22.1 km] **Centro** 3.1
VILA do CONDE
Rua Francisco G. Mosteiró

Santa Clara

Azurara

Azurara

Praia da Árvore
Árvore 2.2   Árvore   Nova
    N-104   **VILARINHO**   0.5 **Albergue**
    N-13   *Asoc.[16]*
    X 3.3   N-104

Praia de Mindelo

Mindelo 3.5   Mindelo   Vairão

    Quinta do Alferes

☎ 252 662 146
Alfaias Q   3.7 **Gião**   Canidelo
Fajozes

Praia de Moreiró
S. Paio 2.7   Moreiró   Modivas
Castro S.Paio

Praia de Labruge   Labruge   **Vilar**

    N-13   1.2 **Alt.** *(metro)*
ques Romanos (réplicas)   *Vilar do Pinheiro*   3.8 **Mosteiró**
Casa do Mar 3.6   Lavra   D

    Santa Marinha   **Gemunde**
    ☎ 229-271-520

Praia da Memória   3.1 **Alt.** *(Moreiras)*
Obelisco 3.7   *Lidador* H   2.9 **Cruce**
    Padrão Moreira   **Industrial Maia I**
    Puma   0.7 **Alt.** *(metro)*
    Pedra H   2.1 **Igreja Maia**
14a Maia – Rates   *Rubras*   C **Fórum Maia**
    IC-24
Praia de Boa Nova   **Ponte Moreiras** 2.1   *Parque Maia*   **MAIA**
central eléctrica
    Custió   ¡perigo!
Capela 3.2   *Farol*   **Araújo** ? 1.2   ← *Ponte Barreiros*
    3.3 ?
Praia Leça da Palmeira   **Leça da Palmeira**   *Mosteiro Leça do Bailo*   [1.1 km]
    Castelo   A-4
Ponte 0.0   B   N-13
MATOSINHOS   Mercado
    Porto Leixões   **Padrão da Légua**   A-3
    A-28
    N-14
    X 2.9   *Circulação*   N-12
    Foz do Douro   *Cintura interna*   IC-23
    Cedofeita   2.2 X ?
    [0.2 km]
W   *Sunset*   Trindade   Campanhã
    PORTO
S   *Sunrise*   São Bento   A 0.0 **Catedral**
    A-1

VILARINHO – BARCELOS

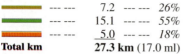

--- ---	7.2	--- ---	26%
--- ---	15.1	--- ---	55%
--- ---	5.0	--- ---	18%
Total km	**27.3 km** (17.0 ml)		

--- --- 28.3 km (+^ 210 m = 1.0 km)

Alto ▲ Goios 150 m (492 ft)

< Ⓐ Ⓗ > Arcos 7.5 km / Rates 11.4 km / Pedra Furada 18.5 km

Monte Franqueira ● *295m*
150m ▲ *Alto (Goios)*
VILARINHO — Arcos — Rates — Pedra Furada — BARCELOS
Río Ave — *Río Este* — *Río Cávado*
0 km — 5 km — 10 km — 15 km — 20 km — 25 km

Stage 15: We finally leave behind the busy roads leading out of Porto and find our first woodland paths around Arcos that bring us through Rates before joining the busy N-306 for a short but dangerous stretch of main road around Pedra Furada. If you took the coastal route to Vila do Conde then take the country roads via Junqueira to rejoin the waymarked route at Arcos. This is a relatively level day's walk with shelter in the woodland areas.

Etapa 15: Por fin dejamos atrás las transitadas carreteras que salen de Oporto y nos encontramos con nuestros primeros senderos dentro del bosque en los alrededores de Arcos, que nos guiarán atravesando Rates antes de llegar a la ajetreada N-306, durante un breve pero peligroso tramo de carretera principal en los alrededores de Pedra Furada. Si tomas la ruta de la costa hasta Vila do Conde, coge después las carreteras rurales vía Junqueira para volver a enlazar con el recorrido marcado en Arcos. La caminata de hoy es relativamente nivelada, y se encuentra refugio en las zonas boscosas.

Etapa 15: Finalmente deixamos para trás as estradas movimentadas que saem do Porto e encontramos os nossos primeiros caminhos de área florestal em redor de Arcos passando por Rates antes de nos juntarmos à movimentada N-306 para um trajecto curto mas perigoso de estrada principal em redor de Pedra Furada. Se escolheram a rota costeira de Vila do Conde sigam as estradas rurais via Junqueira para se juntarem à rota assinalada em Arcos. A caminhada deste dia é relativamente plana com abrigo nas áreas florestais.

Etappe 15: Endlich lassen wir die verkehrsreichen, aus Porto hinausführenden Straßen hinter uns und treffen auf unsere ersten Waldwege in der Nähe von Arcos. Sie führen uns durch Rates, bis wir uns für eine kurze, aber gefährliche Strecke der belebten Hauptstraße N-306 um Pedra Furada anschließen müssen. Wenn Sie die Küstenstraße nach Vila do Conde genommen haben, wählen Sie nun die Landstraßen Richtung Junqueira, um die ausgeschilderte Route in Arcos wieder aufzunehmen. Diese Tageswanderung folgt einer relativ ebenen Strecke und bietet Wetterschutz in den Waldgebieten.

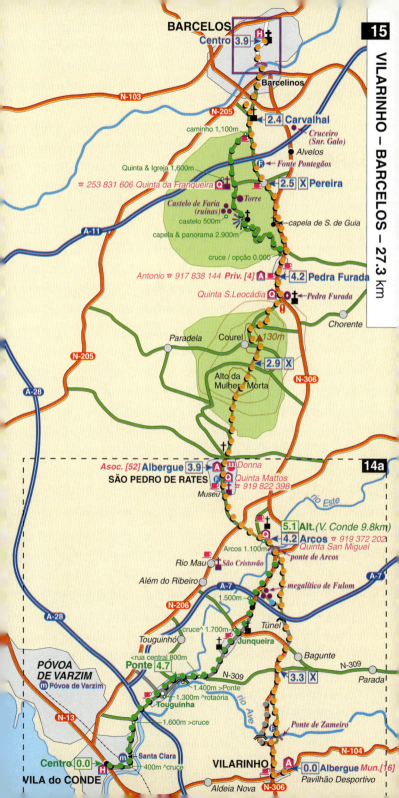

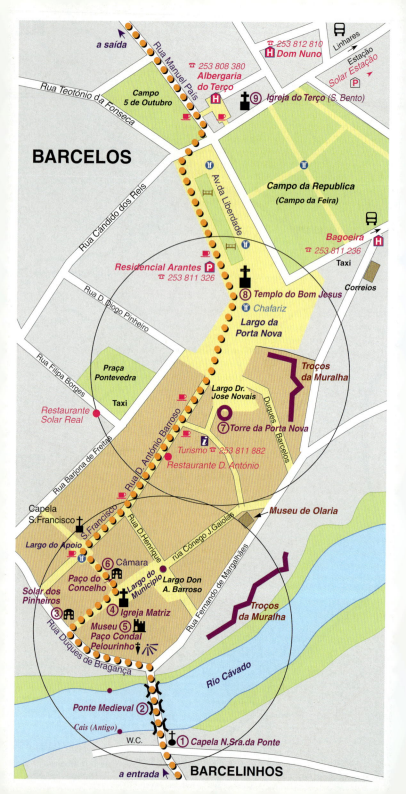

Barcelos: A delightful town on the banks of the rio Cávado with many historic connections to the medieval pilgrimage. The main pedestrian shopping street is part of the camino and leads to the beautiful octagonal *Igreja do Bom Jesus da Cruz* in Largo da Porto Nova which adjoins the extensive market square, home to one of Portugal's best-known markets *Feira de Barcelos* every Thursday. The town is also famous for the 'miracle of the hanged pilgrim' and 'Barcelos Cock', which is also the logo for Portuguese tourism. The main sites are shown on the town plan opposite. There are regular buses to Braga, Portugal's ecclesiastical 'capital' but this would require an extra day. Note the next stage to Ponte de Lima is a very long day requiring an early start (unless you plan staying at the new pilgrim hostel at Tamel S. Pedro Fins).

Barcelos: Una preciosa ciudad situada en la ribera del río Cávado, con muchas relaciones históricas con las peregrinaciones medievales. La calle peatonal comercial más importante forma parte del camino, y lleva a la hermosa iglesia de planta octogonal Igreja do Bom Jesus da Cruz, en Largo da Porta Nova, situado al lado de la amplia plaza del mercado, que cada jueves alberga uno de los mercados más conocidos de Portugal, la Feira de Barcelos. La ciudad es también famosa por el «milagro del peregrino ahorcado» y el «gallo de Barcelos», que es también el símbolo del turismo en Portugal. En el plano de la ciudad se muestran los principales lugares de interés. Hay autobuses regulares hacia Braga, la «capital» eclesiástica de Portugal, pero esta visita requeriría un día extra. Se ha de tener en cuenta que la siguiente etapa, hasta Ponte de Lima, es un día muy largo que precisa un comienzo temprano (a no ser que tengas planeado dormir en el nuevo albergue de peregrinos de Tamel S. Pedro Fins).

Barcelos: Uma cidade encantadora na margem do rio Cávado com muitas ligações históricas à peregrinação medieval. A rua comercial principal pedestre é parte do caminho e leva-nos à octogonal e linda *Igreja do Bom Jesus da Cruz* no Largo da Porta Nova junto à praça enorme do mercado, onde se realiza às quintas-feiras uma das feiras mais conhecidas de Portugal a *Feira de Barcelos*. A cidade também é famosa pelo "milagre do peregrino enforcado" e o "Galo de Barcelos", que é também o logo do turismo de Portugal. Os locais principais estão indicados no plano da cidade em frente. Há um horário regular de autocarros para Braga, a "capital" eclesiástica de Portugal mas para isso é necessário mais um dia. Note-se que a etapa seguinte para Ponte de Lima é um dia muito longo e requer uma partida cedo (a não ser que planeiem ficar na pousada nova para peregrinos em Tamel S. Pedro Fins).

Barcelos: Eine reizvolle Stadt an den Ufern des Flusses Cávado mit vielen historischen Verbindungen zum mittelalterlichen Pilgertum. Die Hauptfußgängerzone und Einkaufsstraße ist ein Teil des Jakobwegs und führt zur schönen achteckigen *Igreja do Bom Jesus da Cruz* in Largo da Porto Nova, die an den ausgedehnten Marktplatz angrenzt. Dieser beherbergt einen von Portugal's bestbekannten Märkten – *Feira de Barcelos* – , der jeden Donnerstag stattfindet. Die Stadt ist ebenfalls bekannt für das 'Wunder des gehängten Pilgers' und den 'Hahn von Barcelos', der auch das Logo für den portugiesischen Tourismus stellt. Die wichtigsten Sehenswürdigkeiten sind auf dem Stadtplan gegenüber verzeichnet. Es gibt regelmäßige Busse nach Braga, Portugals kirchlicher 'Hauptstadt', doch dies würde einen weiteren Tag erfordern. Achtung: Die nächste Etappe nach Ponte de Lima ist ein sehr langer Tagesmarsch, der einen frühen Start erforderlich macht (sofern Sie nicht planen, in der neuen Pilgerherberge in Tamel São Pedro Fins zu übernachten).

BARCELOS – PONTE DE LIMA

--- ---	15.7	--- ---	47%
--- ---	15.8	--- ---	47%
--- ---	2.1	--- ---	6%
Total km	**33.6 km** (20.9 ml)		

--- --- 38.8 km (+^ 440m = 2.2 km)

Alto ▲ Alto da Portela 170 m (558 ft)

< Ⓐ Ⓗ > Portela 9.4 km / Lugar do Corgo 19.1 km

Stage 16: This is one of the longest stages but also one of the most beautiful as we pass along the river Neiva and down into the incomparable beauty of the river Lima valley. However this requires climbing over two hill passes *portelas* one at each end of this stage. The climb up to Alto da Portela at the start is particularly steep. Facilities along this stretch are limited so fill up with water and bring something to eat before setting out for the day.

Etapa 16: Esta es una de las etapas más largas, pero también una de las más hermosas, ya que hacemos el recorrido del río Neiva y descendemos hasta la incomparable belleza del valle del río Lima. Aún así, esto requiere subir dos pasos de montaña, *portelas*, uno a cada extremo de la etapa. La subida al Alto da Portela es especialmente pronunciada al principio. Los servicios a lo largo de este tramo son limitados, así que provéete bien de agua y comida antes de partir.

Etapa 16: Esta é uma das etapas mais longas mas também uma das mais lindas ao longo do rio Neiva e descendo para a beleza incomparável do vale do rio Lima. No entanto, isto requer a subida de duas *portelas*, uma de cada lado da etapa. A subida ao Alto da Portela, é particularmente íngreme no início. Os serviços ao longo deste percurso são limitados portanto abasteçam-se com água e comida antes de começarem a jornada.

Etappe 16: Dies ist einer der längsten Abschnitte, doch auch einer der schönsten, in dem wir den Fluss Neiva entlang und hinunter in die unvergleichbare Schönheit des Flusstals der Lima wandern. Allerdings müssen wir hierfür zwei Hügelpässe – *portelas* – erklimmen, einen an jedem Ende dieser Strecke. Der Anstieg zum Alto da Portela zu Beginn ist besonders steil. Einkaufs- und Verpflegungsmöglichkeiten entlang dieser Strecke sind begrenzt, daher füllen Sie Ihre Wasservorräte auf und packen Sie Verpflegung ein, bevor Sie diese Tageswanderung beginnen.

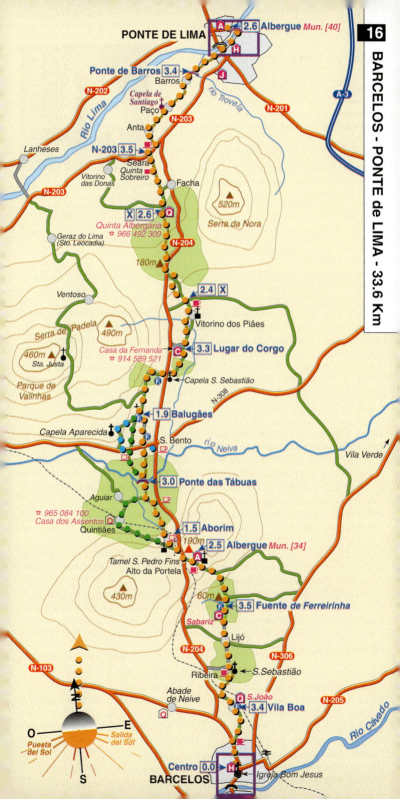

PONTE DE LIMA

A | 2.6 Albergue *Mun.* [40]
H
J

Ponte de Barros | 3.4
Barros

Capela de Santiago
Paço
N-203

Anta

N-202
Rio Lima
Lanheses

N-203 | 3.5

Seara
Quinta Sobreiro
Vitorino das Donas
N-203

Facha

X | 2.6
Q

Quinta Albergaria
☎ 966 492 309
Geraz do Lima
(Sto. Leocadia)

520m
Serra da Nora

N-204
180m▲

Ventoso

2.4 | X

Serra de Padela
490m▲

460m▲
Sta. Justa

Vitorino dos Piâes

Casa da Fernanda
☎ 914 589 521
C | 3.3 Lugar do Corgo

Parque de Valinhas

F
Capela S. Sebastião

N-308

F | 1.9 Balugâes

Capela Aparecida
F
S. Bento

río Neiva

Vila Verde →

3.0 | Ponte das Tábuas

Aguiar

☎ 965 084 100
Casa dos Assentos
Quintiães

1.5 | Aborim
190m▲

2.5 | Albergue *Mun.* [34]
A

Tamel S. Pedro Fins
Alto da Portela

430m▲

60m▲

C | 3.5 Fuente *de* Ferreirinha
Sabariz

Lijó
N-204
N-306

Ribeira
S.Sebastião

Abade de Neive
Q

N-103

Q | S.João
3.4 | Vila Boa
N-205

Rio Cávado

O ——— E

Puesta del Sol
Salida del Sōl

S

Centro | 0.0
H
BARCELOS
Igreja Bom Jesus

PONTE DE LIMA – RUBIÃES

--- ---	10.3	--- ---	57%	
--- ---	7.8	--- ---	43%	
--- ---	0.0	--- ---	0%	
Total km	**18.1 km** (11.2 ml)			

--- ---   20.4 km (+^ 460 m = 2.3 km)

Alto ▲   Portela Grande 405 m (1,329 ft)

Stage 17: We now have our first glorious day where natural pathways account for over half the way and there are no main roads at all. While this is a relatively short stage it also marks our steepest accumulative climb – so prepare for the long ascent up the beautiful Labruja valley, marred only by the presence of the A-3 motorway at the beginning. We finally pass over and into the Coura valley via the Portela Grande. There is reasonable shelter amongst the lovely pinewoods on either side of the pass and a few drinking fonts along the way – you will need to use them!

Etapa 17: Este será nuestro primer día glorioso, en el que más de la mitad del camino consistirá en senderos naturales y no hay ni una sola carretera principal. Aunque es una etapa relativamente corta, también marca nuestra subida acumulativa más pronunciada, así que prepárate para la larga ascensión por el hermoso valle Labruja, arruinada tan solo por la presencia de la autopista A-3 al comienzo. Para terminar pasaremos sobre y dentro del valle del Coura, a través de la Portela Grande. Los encantadores pinos ofrecen un cobijo razonable a cada lado del paso y hay unas cuantas fuentes a lo largo del camino: ¡las necesitarás!

Etapa 17: Temos agora o nosso primeiro dia glorioso no qual os caminhos naturais fazem parte de mais de metade do percurso e não há nenhumas estradas principais. Embora seja uma etapa relativamente curta é também uma das nossas subidas mais íngremes – preparem-se para a subida longa do vale lindo de Labruja, afectada só pela presença da auto-estrada A-3 no início. Passamos esta zona finalmente e entramos no vale de Coura pela Portela Grande. Existe abrigo razoável entre os pinhais agradáveis que se encontram dos dois lados da passagem e algumas fontes pelo caminho – irão precisar de usá-las!

Etappe 17: Jetzt haben wir unseren ersten herrlichen Tag, an dem wir uns mehr als die Hälfte des Weges auf natürlichen Wegen befinden und wo es überhaupt keine Hauptstraßen gibt. Dies ist eine relativ kurze Etappe, doch zeichnet sie sich auch durch den steilsten zunehmenden Anstieg aus – bereiten Sie sich also auf den langen Aufstieg das schöne Labruja-Tal hinauf vor, der nur zu Beginn durch die Autobahn A-3 gestört wird. Schließlich überqueren wir den Pass, Portela Grande, in das Coura Tal hinein. Es gibt ausreichend Wetterschutz in den herrlichen Nadelwäldern beidseits des Passes und ein paar Trinkbrunnen auf dem Weg – Sie werden Sie brauchen!

RUBIÃES

Milário → ✝ S.Pedro Rubiães
1.3 Albergue ◀

Pensão São Roque ☎ 252 943 692
3.7 São Roque ◀
Agualonga

Coura

→ Ponte Romano

N-201

Cabanas
Antigo molinho
Morgado
Romarigães

405m **3.1** Alto *Portela Grande* ◀

435m

Cruz dos Franceses

▲ 530m

520m

✝ *Santuário*
Labruja
EN-306

135m
1.8 Fonte *Três Bicas* ◀

Capela N.S. Nieves
2.9 Café *Nunes* ◀
Revolta
Ponte do Arco

A-3 Ponte **2.6**
S. Pedro

▲ 720m

rio Labruja
N-201

EN-306
café 200m
Calheiros

Ponte Arco
da Geia

EN-306
A-27
2.7 Igreja ◀
Arcozelo

A-3

Casa de Sabadão
Q

O
o por do sol

E
o nascer do sol

S

Quinta Arquino
Q

A-27

A **0.0** Albergue ◀

PONTE de LIMA

RUBIÃES – VALENÇA / TUI

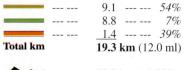

--- ---	9.1 --- ---	*54%*
--- ---	8.8 --- ---	*7%*
--- ---	1.4 --- ---	*39%*
Total km	**19.3 km** (12.0 ml)	

--- --- 20.3 km (+^ 200 m = 1.0 km)

Alto ▲ S. Bento 270 m (886 ft)

Stage 18: Apart from the short stretch of main road through Valença into Tui the rest of this stage is split between natural pathways and quiet country roads, much of it through woodland affording shelter from rain or sun. Except a modest climb out of the Coura river valley the majority of this stage is downhill from S. Roque. The Minho now becomes the Miño and our clocks also need adjusting one hour as we make our way over the border from Portugal into Spain. There are pilgrim hostels in both Valença and Tui (see town plans).

Etapa 18: Aparte del breve tramo de carretera principal que atraviesa Valença para llegar a Tui, el resto de esta etapa se reparte entre senderos naturales y tranquilas carreteras rurales. Una buena parte discurre entre bosques que proporcionan cobijo de la lluvia y el sol. A excepción de una modesta subida para salir del valle del río Coura, la mayor parte de esta etapa es cuesta abajo desde S. Roque. El Minho se convierte ahora en el Miño, y los relojes también necesitan un ajuste de una hora mientras atravesamos la frontera entre Portugal y España. Hay albergues de peregrinos tanto en Valença como en Tui (ver los planos de ciudad).

Etapa 18: Para além do percurso curto de estrada principal por Valença até Tui o resto desta etapa é dividido entre caminhos naturais e estradas rurais sossegadas, na sua maioria através de áreas florestais dando-nos abrigo da chuva e do sol. Excepto pela subida moderada para sair do vale de Coura a maior parte desta etapa é uma descida depois de S. Roque. O Minho torna-se o Miño e os nossos relógios poderão necessitar de serem ajustados uma hora ao passarmos a fronteira de Portugal para Espanha. Existem pousadas para peregrinos em Valença e Tui. (ver plano da cidade).

Etappe 18: Abgesehen von dem kurzen Abschnitt Hauptstraße durch Valença nach Tui teilt sich der Rest dieser Etappe auf natürliche Wege und ruhige Landstraßen auf, viel davon durch Waldgebiet, das Schutz vor Regen oder Sonne bietet. Außer einem moderaten Aufstieg vom Flusstal des Coura herauf geht es den Großteil der Strecke von São Roque bergab. Der Minho wird nun zum Miño und möglicherweise müssen wir auch unsere Uhren um eine Stunde vor- oder zurückstellen, während wir die Grenze von Portugal nach Spanien überqueren. Sowohl in Valença wie auch in Tui gibt es Pilgerherbergen (siehe Stadtpläne).

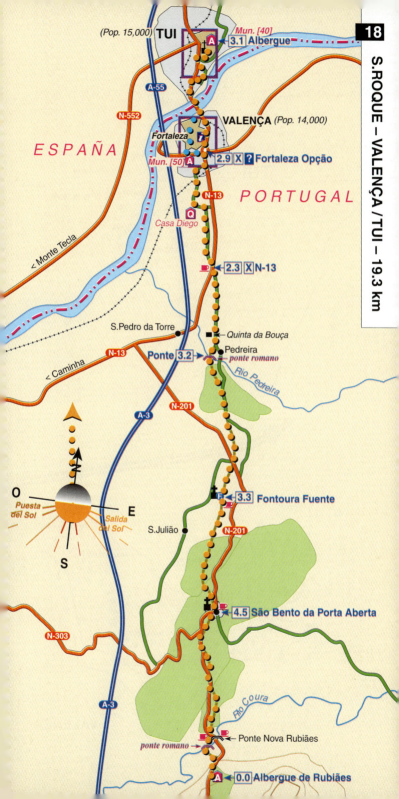

(Pop. 15,000) **TUI**

Mun. [40]
3.1 Albergue

A-55

N-552

VALENÇA (Pop. 14,000)

E S P A Ñ A

Fortaleza

Mun. [50] A **2.9** X **? Fortaleza Opção**

P O R T U G A L

N-13

< Monte Tecla

Q
Casa Diego

2.3 X **N-13**

S.Pedro da Torre
■ ← *Quinta da Bouça*

N-13
Ponte 3.2 → *ponte romano*
● Pedreira

< Caminha

Rio Pedreira

N-201

A-3

3.3 Fontoura Fuente

S.Julião ●
N-201

O
Puesta del Sol

E
Salida del Sol

S

■† **4.5 São Bento da Porta Aberta**

N-303

A-3

Rio C. oura

ponte romano → **Ponte Nova Rubiães**

A **0.0 Albergue de Rubiães**

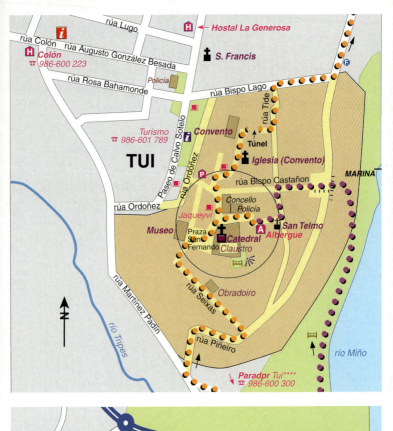

rúa Lugo

rúa Colón

rúa Augusto González Besada

Hostal La Generosa

Colón
☎ 986-600 223

S. Francis

rúa Rosa Bahamonde

Policía

rúa Bispo Lago

rúa Tide

Turismo
☎ 986-601 789

Convento

Túnel

TUI

Iglesia (Convento)

Paseo de Calvo Sotelo

rúa Ordóñez

rúa Bispo Castañón

MARINA

Concello
Policía

rúa Ordoñez

Museo

Jaqueyvi

Praza
San
Fernando

Catedral

San Telmo

A

Albergue

Claustro

rúa Martínez Padín

rúa Seixas

Obradoiro

N

río Tripes

rúa Piñeiro

río Miño

Paradpr Tui**
☎ 986-600 300

A-1

N

Mun. São Teotónio
[50]
A

☎ 251-800 260
Pousada Teotonio

Casa do Poço
☎ 251-825 235

**Baluarte
do Socorro**

Lara
H

☎ 251-824 348

Av. dos Bombeiros Voluntários

Fortaleza

Misericórdia
H

Matriz
P

**Val
Flores**
H

☎ 251-824 106

**LargoDr.A
Guimarães**

Bom Jesus
Bom Jesus

Portas
do Máio

**Praça
República**

S. Estevão
Miliario

Portas
da Coroada

San Sebastião

**Largo da
Trapichara**

Av. de Espanha

Portas
do Sol

Minho

Antás
Estação

Av. Tio Fontes

☎ 251-822 580
P Ponte Seca

i Turismo

VALENÇA

Valença: if you intend to stay in the pilgrim hostel and/or visit the atmospheric old fort with its colourful markets and restaurants, veer left at the roundabout and make your way uphill 200m to *albergue* (left) and entrance to the *fortaleza* (right). Continue through the fort and down the steps at the far end to rejoin the waymarked route just before the bridge over the river Minho. **Tui:** the hostel adjoins the cathedral in the historic old quarter. This is the main starting point for Spanish pilgrims but spaces are held in the hostel until late afternoon for those walking from Portugal. The cathedral has a chapel dedicated to St. James and a peaceful garden off the cloisters with beautiful views over the river.

Valença: si tu intención es alojarte en el albergue para peregrinos y/o visitar la antigua fortaleza, con sus coloridos mercados y restaurantes, gira a la izquierda en la rotonda y asciende unos 200 m hasta el albergue (izquierda) y la entrada a «la Fortaleza» (derecha). Continua a través de esta y baja las escaleras que hay al otro lado para volver a encontrar el recorrido marcado, justo antes del puente sobre el río Minho. **Tui:** el albergue está junto a la catedral, en el casco antiguo. Este es el principal punto de partida de los peregrinos españoles, pero se guarda sitio en el albergue hasta entrada la tarde para quienes vengan caminando desde Portugal. En la catedral hay una capilla dedicada a Santiago y un jardín lleno de paz que da a los claustros, con unas hermosas vistas al río.

Valença: se tenciona ficar na pousada para peregrinos e / ou visitar o pitoresco antigo forte com os seus mercados e restaurantes coloridos, vire à esquerda na rotunda e suba os 200m para o albergue (esquerda) e entrada para a fortaleza (direita). Continue pelo forte e desça as escadas para voltar à rota assinalada mesmo antes da ponte sobre o rio Minho. **Tui:** a pousada está adjacente à catedral no bairro histórico antigo. Este é o ponto de partida principal para os peregrinos Espanhóis mas são guardados lugares na pousada, até anoitecer, para os caminhantes vindos de Portugal. A catedral tem uma capela dedicada a S. Tiago e um jardim tranquilo fora dos claustros com vistas lindas para o rio.

Valença: Wenn Sie beabsichtigen, in der Pilgerherberge zu übernachten und/oder das stimmungsvolle alte Kastell mit seinen farbenprächtigen Märkten und Restaurants zu besichtigen, biegen Sie links am Kreisverkehr ab und gehen Sie 200 m den Berg hinauf bis zur Albergue (links) und dem Eingang zum Fortaleza (rechts). Gehen Sie durch das Kastell hindurch und die Treppen am anderen Ende hinunter, um die ausgeschilderte Route kurz vor der Brücke über den Fluss Minho wieder aufzunehmen. **Tui:** Die Herberge liegt neben der Kathedrale im historischen alten Viertel. Dies ist der wichtigste Ausgangspunkt für spanische Pilger, doch bis zum späten Nachmittag werden in der Herberge Plätze für diejenigen freigehalten, die von Portugal aus wandern. Die Kathedrale besitzt eine Kapelle, die dem heiligen Jakobus gewidmet ist, sowie einen friedlichen Garten jenseits der Kreuzgänge, mit wunderbarem Blick über den Fluss.

VALENÇA / TUI – REDONDELA

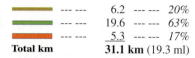

		6.2	--- ---	20%
	--- ---	19.6	--- ---	63%
	--- ---	5.3	--- ---	17%

Total km **31.1 km** (19.3 ml)

--- --- 32.6 km (+^ 300 m = 1.5 km)
Alto ▲ Alto Cornedo 235 m (771 ft)
< Ⓐ Ⓗ > Porriño 16.2 km / Mos 21.5 km

Stage 19: Most of this stage is along quiet country roads and woodland paths. The challenge today is the long slog through the industrial estates around Porriño and the busy N-550, which we have to cross several times. There is also a steep climb from Mos up the 'Road of the Knights' *Rúa dos Cabaleiros* and up again to Monte Cornedo. However, this is rewarded by our first views of the sea since leaving Porto, the Ría de Vigo. The final part of the day is then all the way downhill into the attractive town of Redondela.

Etapa 19: La mayor parte de esta etapa discurre por tranquilas carreteras rurales y senderos de bosque. El reto de hoy es el largo y duro paso a través de las naves industriales de Porriño y la transitada N-550, que tendremos que cruzar varias veces. También hay una pronunciada subida desde Mos por la calle de los caballeros, *Rúa dos Cabaleiros*, y de nuevo hacia arriba hasta Monte Cornedo. De todas maneras, la recompensa son las primeras vistas del mar desde que partimos de Oporto, la ría de Vigo. La parte final del día es el descenso por la montaña hasta el atractivo pueblo de Redondela.

Etapa 19: A maior parte desta etapa é por estradas rurais sossegadas e caminhos florestais. O desafio hoje é a caminhada fatigante através das zonas industriais em redor de Porriño e a movimentada N-550, que temos de atravessar várias vezes. Há também uma subida íngreme de Mos pela *Rua dos Cabaleiros* e novamente até ao Monte Cornedo. No entanto, isto é recompensado com as nossas primeiras vistas do mar desde que deixámos o Porto, a Ría de Vigo. A parte final do dia é a descida para a atraente cidade de Redondela.

Etappe 19: Der größte Teil dieser Etappe verläuft entlang ruhiger Landstraßen und Waldpfade. Die heutige Herausforderung ist der lange Kampf durch die Industriegebiete um Porriño und die verkehrsreiche N-550, die wir mehrfach überqueren müssen. Auch gibt es einen steilen Anstieg von Mos die 'Straße der Ritter" – *Rúa dos Cabaleiros* – und zum Monte Cornedo hinauf. Allerdings wird dies mit unseren ersten Ausblicken auf das Meer seit dem Verlassen von Porto belohnt, der Ría de Vigo. Der letzte Teilabschnitt des Tages führt dann den ganzen Weg bergab in die reizvolle Stadt von Redondela.

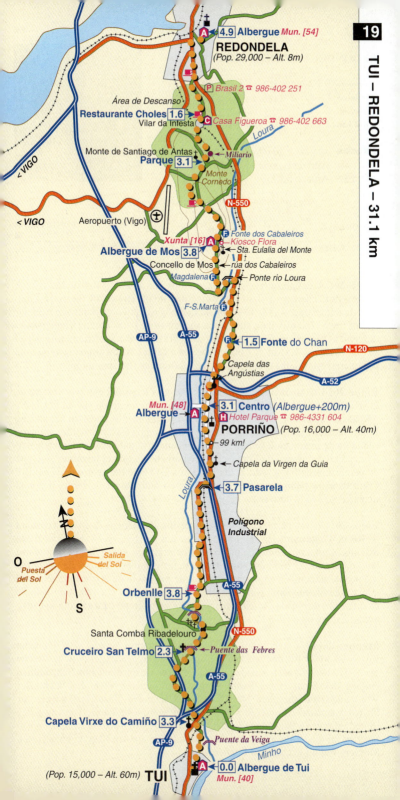

Ⓐ 4.9 **Albergue** *Mun. [54]*
REDONDELA
(Pop. 29,000 – Alt. 8m)

Ⓟ *Brasil 2* ☎ 986-402 251

Área de Descanso
Restaurante Choles 1.6
Vilar da Infesta
Ⓒ *Casa Figueroa* ☎ 986-402 663

Monte de Santiago de Antas
Parque 3.1
Miliario
Monte Cornedo

N-550

Aeropuerto (Vigo)

Ⓕ *Fonte dos Cabaleiros*
Xunta [16] Ⓐ ← *Kiosco Flora*
Albergue de Mos 3.8 ← Sta. Eulalia del Monte
Concello de Mos ← *rúa dos Cabaleiros*
Magdalena Ⓕ ← *Ponte rio Loura*

F-S.Marta Ⓕ

AP-9 A-55
Ⓕ 1.5 **Fonte do Chan** N-120

Capela das Angústias
A-52

Mun. [48]
Albergue Ⓐ 3.1 **Centro** (Albergue+200m)
Ⓗ *Hotel Parque* ☎ 986-4331 604
PORRIÑO (Pop. 16,000 – Alt. 40m)
← *99 km!*
← *Capela da Virgen da Guia*

3.7 **Pasarela**

Polígono Industrial

Loura

A-55

O
Salida del Sol
Puesta del Sol
S

Orbenlle 3.8

Santa Comba Ribadelouro
N-550

Cruceiro San Telmo 2.3 ← *Puente das Febres*

A-55

Capela Virxe do Camiño 3.3
AP-9
Puente da Veiga
Minho

(Pop. 15,000 – Alt. 60m)
TUI Ⓐ 0.0 **Albergue de Tui**
Mun. [40]

REDONDELA – PONTEVEDRA

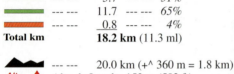

		5.7	--- ---	*31%*
		11.7	--- ---	*65%*
		0.8	--- ---	*4%*
Total km		**18.2 km** (11.3 ml)		

--- ---   20.0 km (+^ 360 m = 1.8 km)

Alto ▲   Alto da Lomba 153 m (502 ft)

< 🅰 🅗 >   Arcade 6.9 km

Stage 20: A delightfully varied stage along the coastal inlet of the Ría de Pontevedra. There is a short but dangerous uphill stretch of the N-550 into Arcade but an opportunity to swim along the beach at Ponte Sampaio at the far end of town. The way then climbs the ancient stone paths around Canicouva to descend to the provincial capital of Pontevedra. Note the modern pilgrim hostel in Pontevedra is 1.5 km *this* side of the town centre. Allow time to explore the old quarter later in the evening or in the morning as you pass through.

Etapa 20: Una maravillosa y variada etapa a lo largo del entrante costero de la ría de Pontevedra. Hay un breve pero peligroso tramo de subida por la N-550 hasta Arcade, pero también tendrás la oportunidad de nadar en la playa en Ponte Sampaio, al final del pueblo. Después el camino asciende por los antiguos senderos de piedra en los alrededores de Canicouva para acabar descendiendo a la capital provincial de Pontevedra. Ten en cuenta que el moderno albergue de peregrinos de Pontevedra está a 1,5 km a este lado del centro de la ciudad. Concédete un tiempo para explorar el casco antiguo por la tarde, o por la mañana cuando lo atravieses.

Etapa 20: Uma etapa agradavelmente diversificada ao longo da enseada costeira da Ría de Pontevedra. Há uma subida curta mas perigosa da N-550 para Arcade mas que é uma oportunidade para nadar na praia em Ponte Sampaio no outro lado da cidade. O caminho sobe depois pelos caminhos antigos de pedra em redor de Canicouva para descer à capital de província de Pontevedra. Note-se que a pousada moderna para peregrinos em Pontevedra é a 1.5km do lado de *cá* do centro da cidade. Adicionem também algum tempo para explorar o bairro antigo à noite ou de manhã ao passarem por ele.

Etappe 20: Eine angenehm variantenreiche Etappe entlang der schmalen Küstenbucht der Ría de Pontevedra. Es gibt eine kurze, aber gefährliche Strecke die N-550 bergauf nach Arcade hinein, aber eine Gelegenheit zum Schwimmen entlang des Strandes bei Ponte Sampaio am anderen Ende der Stadt. Der Weg steigt dann die alten Steinpfade um Canicouva hinauf, um wieder zur Provinzhauptstadt Pontevedra hinunterzuführen. Achtung: Die moderne Pilgerherberge in Pontevedra liegt 1.5 km diesseits des Stadtzentrums. Planen Sie Zeit für die Erforschung des alten Viertels ein, am Abend oder am nächsten Morgen, wenn Sie hindurch wandern.

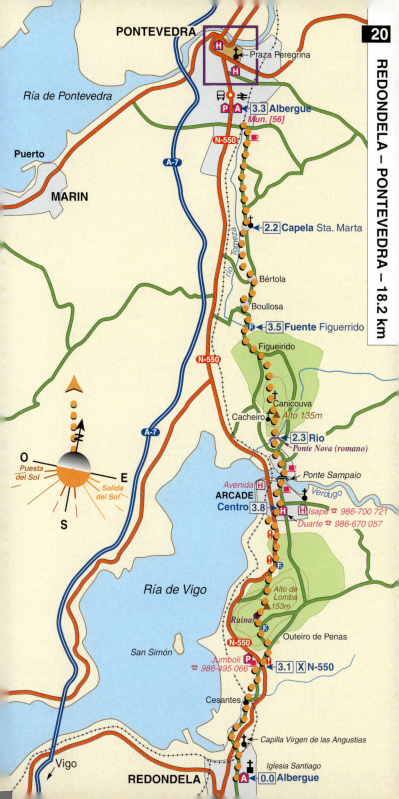

PONTEVEDRA

[H] · Praza Peregrina

[H]

[P] [A] **3.3 Albergue**
Mun. [56]

Ría de Pontevedra

Puerto

MARIN

N-550

[A-7]

2.2 Capela Sta. Marta

Bértola

Boullosa

[F] **3.5 Fuente** Figuerrido

Figueirido

N-550

Canicouva
Cacheiro · *Alto 135m*

[A-7]

2.3 Rio
Ponte Nova (romano)

Ponte Sampaio

Avenida [H] · *Verdugo*

ARCADE
Centro **3.8**

[H] [H] Isape ☎ 986-700 721
Duarte ☎ 986-670 057

[F]

Alto de Lomba 153m

Ría de Vigo

Ruinas

[F]

Outeiro de Penas

N-550

San Simón

Jumboli
☎ 986-495 066
[P] **3.1** [X] **N-550**

Cesantes

O *Puesta del Sol*
E *Salida del Sol*
S

† *Capilla Virgen de las Angustias*

† *Iglesia Santiago*

Vigo

REDONDELA
[A] **0.0 Albergue**

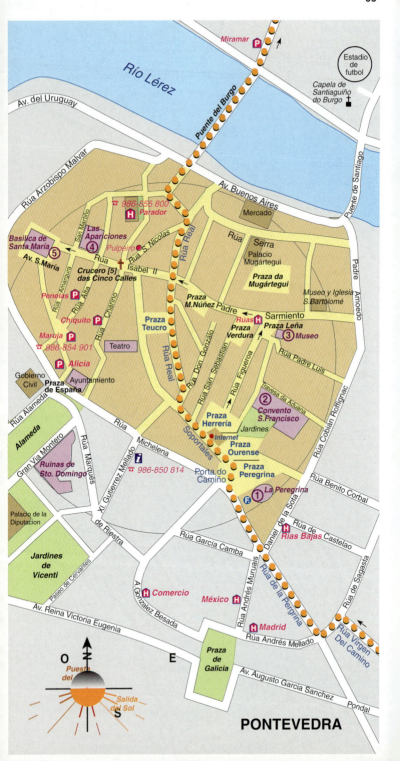

Río Lérez

Miramar

Av. del Uruguay

Estadio
de
futbol

Capela de
Santiaguiño
do Burgo

Puente del Burgo

Av. Buenos Aires

Puente de Santiago

Mercado

☎ 986-855 800
Parador

Rúa Arzobispo Malvar

Las
Apariciones

Basílica de
Santa María

Pulpeiro

Rúa S. Nicolás

Rúa

Serra

Palacio
Mugártegui

Rúa Real

Padre Amoedo

Av. S.María

Rúa
Isabel II

Crucero [5]
das Cinco Calles

Praza da
Mugártegui

Museo y Iglesia
S.Bartolomé

Penelas

Praza
M.Núñez Padre

Rúas

Sarmiento

Chiquito

Praza
Teucro

Praza
Verdura

Praza Leña

Museo

Maruja
☎ 986-854 901

Teatro

Rúa Don Gonzalo

Rúa San Sebastián

Rúa Figueroa

Rúa Padre Luís

Alicia

Rúa Real

Gobierno
Civil

Ayuntamiento

Travesía da Aduana

Convento
S.Francisco

Rúa Cobián Roffignac

Praza
de España

Soportales

Praza
Herrería

Jardines

Rúa

Alameda

Gran Vía Montero

Rúa Marqués

Michelena

Internet

Praza
Ourense

Rúa Benito Corbal

Ruinas de
Sto. Domingo

X. Gutierrez Mellado

☎ 986-850 814

Porta do
Camiño

Praza
Peregrina

Palacio de la
Diputación

de Riestra

La Peregrina

Daniel de la Sota

Rúa de
Castelao

Rías Bajas

Jardines
de
Vicenti

Paseo de Cérvantes

Rúa García Camba

Rúa de Sagasta

Comercio

México

Rúa Andrés Muruais

Rúa de la Peregrina

Av. Reina Victoria Eugenia

A González Besada

Madrid

Rúa Virgen
Del Camino

Praza
de
Galicia

Rúa Andrés Mellado

O

E

N

Puesta
del

Av. Augusto García Sanchez

Pondal

Salida
del Sol

S

PONTEVEDRA

Pontevedra is the provincial capital with extensive commercial activity. At the heart of its modern suburbs is a delightful medieval core *zona monumental / barrio antigua*. The waymarked route follows the original camino *Rúa Real* that goes right through the centre of the ancient quarter. The main sites are listed on the town plan opposite, starting at the *Porta do Camiño* and XVIIth century pilgrim chapel *Santuario de la Peregrina* built to a floor plan in the shape of a scallop shell. Praza de Leña is a typical Galician square with squat granite arcades and central *cruceiro* and the adjoining *Museo de Pontevedra* houses a collection of images of St. James dating from XIIth century. At the far end of town is the Basilica de Santa María A Grande whose southern façade is a storybook in stone, reminiscent of some of the craftsmanship that adorns Santiago cathedral.

Pontevedra es la capital de provincia, y posee una gran actividad comercial. En el interior de sus modernas afueras se encuentra un maravilloso corazón medieval, la zona monumental o barrio antiguo. El recorrido marcado sigue el camino original por la Rúa Real, que atraviesa el centro del casco antiguo. Los principales lugares de interés están listados en el plano de la ciudad, comenzando por la Porta do Camiño y la capilla de peregrinos del siglo XVII Santuario da Peregrina, construido sobre una planta con forma de concha de vieira. La Praza da Leña es una típica plaza gallega con achaparrados soportales de granito y un *cruceiro* central. El adyacente Museo de Pontevedra alberga una colección de imágenes de Santiago que datan del siglo XII. Al final de la ciudad se encuentra la Basílica de Santa María A Grande, cuya fachada sur es un relato en piedra que recuerda a ciertas artesanías que adornan la catedral de Santiago.

Pontevedra é uma capital de província com uma actividade comercial extensa. No centro dos seus subúrbios modernos encontra-se um fulcro medieval encantador *zona monumental / barrio antigua*. A rota assinalada segue o caminho original *Rua Real* que passa pelo centro do bairro antigo. Os locais principais estão indicados no plano da cidade em frente, começando na *Porta do Camiño* e na capela dos peregrinos do século XVII *Santuário de la Peregrina* cuja planta é em forma de concha. Praza de Leña é um largo típico galego com arcadas atarracadas e em granito e *cruceiro* central, o adjacente *Museo de Pontevedra* tem uma colecção de imagens de S. Tiago datadas do século XII. No outro lado da cidade está a Basílica de Santa Maria A Grande cuja fachada sul é um livro de histórias em pedra relembrando em parte o estilo artesanal que adorna a catedral de Santiago.

Pontevedra ist die Provinzhauptstadt mit ausgedehnter Handelsaktivität. Im Zentrum ihrer modernen Vororte findet sich ein reizvoller mittelalterlicher Kern, *zona monumental / barrio antigua*. Die ausgeschilderte Route folgt dem ursprünglichen Jakobsweg, *Rúa Real*, der mitten durch das Zentrum des alten Viertels führt. Die wichtigsten Sehenswürdigkeiten sind auf dem Stadtplan auf der Seite gegenüber aufgelistet, beginnend an der *Porta do Camiño* und der Pilgerkapelle des 17. Jahrhunderts, *Santuario de la Peregrina,* die nach einem Bodenplan in Form einer Jakobsmuschel gebaut wurde. Praza de Leña ist ein typisch galicischer Platz mit gedrungenen Granit-Arkaden und zentralem *cruceiro,* und das angrenzende *Museo de Pontevedra* beherbergt eine Sammlung von Abbildungen des Heiligen Jakobus, die auf das 12. Jahrhundert zurückgeht. Am anderen Ende der Stadt befindet sich die Basilica de Santa María A Grande, deren südliche Fassade ein in Stein gehauenes Bilderbuch ist, das an Aspekte der Handwerkskunst erinnert, die die Santiago-Kathedrale schmückt.

PONTEVEDRA – CALDAS DE REIS

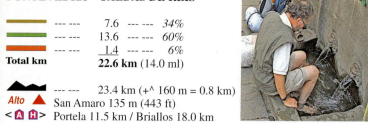

--- ---	7.6	--- ---	*34%*
--- ---	13.6	--- ---	*60%*
--- ---	1.4	--- ---	*6%*
Total km	**22.6 km** (14.0 ml)		

▰ --- --- 23.4 km (+^ 160 m = 0.8 km)

Alto ▲ San Amaro 135 m (443 ft)

< Ⓐ Ⓗ > Portela 11.5 km / Briallos 18.0 km

100m | *135m* ▲San Mauro
Albergue San Mauro
■PONTEVEDRA Briallos **CALDAS**
Río Barosa
0 km — 5 km — 10 km — 15 km — 20 km

Stage 21: A third of this stage is along woodland paths as we follow a shallow river valley crossing the railway on several occasions. There is little elevation apart from a gentle climb around San Amaro. Approaching Caldas de Reis we hop on and off the N-555 a few times but the stretches are short with good visability. Facilities en route are limited but there are good services in Caldas including the hot springs from which the town derives its name (see town plan).

Etapa 21: Un tercio de esta etapa transcurre por senderos entre bosques, mientras seguimos un valle de río poco profundo, cruzando en varias ocasiones la vía del tren. La altura es escasa, aparte de una suave subida cerca de San Amaro. Cuando nos acercamos a Caldas de Reis hemos de entrar y salir de la N-555 unas cuantas veces, pero son tramos cortos y con buena visibilidad. Los servicios a lo largo del recorrido son limitados, pero en Caldas hay una gran oferta, entre la que se encuentran las fuentes calientes de las que toma su nombre el pueblo (ver plano).

Etapa 21: Um terço desta etapa é através de carreiros florestais enquanto seguimos um vale de rio pouco fundo atravessando a via-férrea em várias ocasiões. Há pouca elevação para além de uma subida suave em volta de San Amaro. Ao aproximarmo-nos de Caldas de Reis entramos e saímos algumas vezes da N-555 mas os percursos são curtos com boa visão. Os serviços nesta rota são limitados mas existem bons serviços em Caldas incluindo as termas das quais o nome da cidade é originário (ver plano da cidade).

Etappe 21: Ein Drittel dieser Strecke führt uns auf Waldpfaden ein flaches Flusstal entlang, wobei wir die Bahngleise mehrfach überqueren. Es gibt wenige Bodenerhebungen, abgesehen von einem sanften Aufstieg um San Amaro. Im Anmarsch auf Caldas de Reis begeben wir uns mehrmals streckenweise auf die N-555, doch die Abschnitte sind kurz und haben gute Seitenmarkierungen. Einkaufs- und Verpflegungsmöglichkeiten auf der Route sind begrenzt, doch Caldas verfügt über gute Einrichtungen, einschließlich der heißen Quellen, die der Stadt ihren Namen geben (siehe Stadtplan).

CALDAS de REIS
(Pop. 7,000 – Alt. 25m)

H

H **1.6** Ponte

río Umia

río Umia

< *Vilagarcía*

Portas

Río Chain

3.0 Tívo

1.2 Rotonda
Cruceiro

A Albergue +½ km
Mun. [28]

A-9

Río Lamas

3.9 N-550 Puente

río Barosa

Cascada y Molinos

*Parque Natural
de Ría Barosa*

Cruceiro de Amonisa
Barro

As Eiras
1.4 **X**

A Albergue +½ km **Mun. [50 suelo]**
San Mamede da Portela

Albergue **?** **X** **1.8**
San Amaro

Fuente San Amaro
Mesón Don Pulpo

4.5 **X** Ferrocarril

O ──── E
*puesta
del Sol*   *salida
del Sol*
S

San Caetano

N-550

3.7 Santa María de Alba

A-9

Río Lerez

Poio

< *Sanxenxo*
C-550

Ourense >

N-541

1.5 Centro

PONTEVEDRA

A **0.0** Albergue

CALDAS DE REIS – PADRÓN

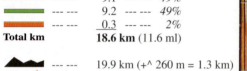

--- ---	9.1	--- ---	49%	
--- ---	9.2	--- ---	49%	
--- ---	0.3	--- ---	2%	
Total km	**18.6 km** (11.6 ml)			

--- ---   19.9 km (+^ 260 m = 1.3 km)

Alto ▲   Cortiñas 160 m (525 ft)

Stage 22: The route is split between woodland pathways and quiet country roads (apart from a short stretch of main road entering Pontecesures). There is a climb up to Cortiñas before descending sharply into the Valga valley and another short ascent to a viewpoint above Pontecesures before crossing the Río Ulla and Sar into Padrón – legendary landing place of Saint James to launch his ministry and, subsequently, the return of his body for burial (see town plan).

Etapa 22: El recorrido se divide entre senderos campestres y tranquilas carreteras rurales, aparte de un breve tramo de carretera principal a la entrada de Pontecesures. Hay una subida hasta Cortiñas antes de descender bruscamente al valle del Valga y otro breve ascenso a un mirador sobre Pontecesures antes de cruzar los ríos Ulla y Sar para entrar a Padrón, el legendario lugar a donde llegó Santiago para comenzar su ministerio y, en consecuencia, el lugar de regreso de su cuerpo para ser enterrado (ver plano de la ciudad).

Etapa 22: A rota é uma combinação entre carreiros florestais e estradas rurais sossegadas (exceptuando um percurso curto de estrada principal ao entrar Pontecesures). Há uma subida para Cortiñas antes de se descer bruscamente para o vale Valga e outra subida curta para um ponto panorâmico acima de Pontecesures antes de se atravessar o Rio Ulla e Sar into Padrón – o local lendário escolhido por S. Tiago para iniciar o seu ministério e, subsequentemente, do regresso do seu corpo para ser sepultado (ver plano da cidade).

Etappe 22: Die Route verteilt sich auf Waldwege und ruhige Landstraßen (abgesehen von einem kurzen Abschnitt auf der Hauptstraße beim Ortseingang von Pontecesures). Es gibt einen Aufstieg nach Cortiñas hinauf, bevor wir steil in das Valga-Tal hinuntersteigen, und einen weiteren kurzen Anstieg zu einem Aussichtspunkt über Pontecesures, bevor wir die Flüsse Ulla und Sar nach Padrón hinein überqueren – legendäre Landestelle des Heiligen Jakobus, von der aus er sein Predigtamt startete und wohin im folgenden auch sein Körper zum Begräbnis zurückgebracht wurde (siehe Stadtplan).

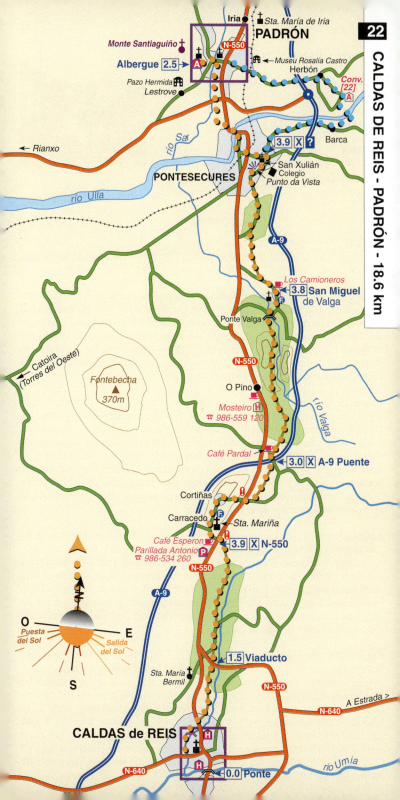

Iria
✝ Sta. María de Iria
PADRÓN

Monte Santiaguiño ✝
N-550
Museu Rosalía Castro
Herbón
Albergue 2.5
A
Conv.
[22]
A
Pazo Hermida
Lestrove

← Rianxo
río Sar
Barca
3.9 X ?
San Xulián
Colegio
PONTESECURES
Punto da Vista
río Ulla

A-9

Los Camioneros
✝ 3.8 San Miguel
de Valga
Ponte Valga

Catoira
(Torres del Oeste)
N-550

Fontebecha
370m
O Pino
Mosteiro H
☎ 986-559 120

Café Pardal
3.0 X A-9 Puente

Cortiñas
Carracedo
Sta. Mariña
Café Esperon
Parillada Antonio
☎ 986-534 260
P
3.9 X N-550
N-550

río Valga

A-9

O
Puesta
del Sol
E
Salida
del Sol
S

1.5 Viaducto
Sta. María
Bermil
N-550
A Estrada >
N-640

CALDAS de REIS
H
H
N-640
0.0 Ponte
río Umia

PADRÓN – SANTIAGO DE COMPOSTELA

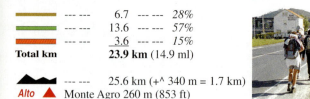

	--- ---	6.7	--- ---	28%	
	--- ---	13.6	--- ---	57%	
	--- ---	3.6	--- ---	15%	
Total km		**23.9 km** (14.9 ml)			

▲▲▲	--- ---	25.6 km (+^ 340 m = 1.7 km)
Alto ▲	Monte Agro 260 m (853 ft)	
< 🅐 🅷 >	Areal 9.1 km / Teo 10.7 km	

Stage 23: A varied day's walk with several stretches on the N-550, which gets increasingly busy as we approach Santiago. However, we still find natural pathways through oak, pine and eucalyptus woodlands around Teo. This stage also has the detour (little visited and not waymarked) to Castro Lupario, a site of Queen Lupa's legendary fortress (add 2 hours for the round trip and time to hack your way through the undergrowth). There are still surprisingly few cafes or shops en route so stock up before leaving Padrón.

Etapa 23: Un día de camino variado, con varios tramos en la N-550, que se va volviendo progresivamente transitada a medida que nos acercamos a Santiago. De todas maneras, todavía hallamos senderos naturales que cruzan bosques de robles, pinos y eucaliptos cerca de Teo. En esta etapa también nos encontramos con el rodeo (escasamente visitado y sin señalización) a Castro Lupario, el lugar en el que se hallaba la legendaria fortaleza de la Reina Lupa (añade dos horas para poder ir y volver y tener tiempo para abrirte paso entre la maleza). Sorprendentemente, todavía hay pocas cafeterías y tiendas en el camino, así que aprovisiónate bien antes de salir de Padrón.

Etapa 23: Um dia de caminhada diversificada com vários percursos pela N-550, que se vai tornando mais movimentada ao aproximarmo-nos de Santiago. No entanto, ainda encontramos caminhos com carvalhos, pinhais e eucaliptais em redor de Teo. Esta etapa também tem um desvio (pouco visitado e não assinalado) para Castro Lupario, lugar da fortaleza lendária de Queen Lupa (acrescentar 2 horas para ida e volta e tempo para cortar caminho através da vegetação). Surpreendentemente ainda há poucos cafés ou lojas na rota por isso abasteçam-se antes de sair de Padrón.

Etappe 23: Eine abwechslungsreiche Tageswanderung mit verschiedenen Teilabschnitten auf der N-550, die zunehmend verkehrsreicher wird, je näher wir an Santiago herankommen. Doch finden wir noch immer natürliche Wanderwege durch Eichen-, Pinien- und Eukalyptuswälder um Teo herum. Dieses Stadium verzeichnet auch einen (wenig besuchten und noch nicht beschilderten) Abstecher nach Castro Lupario, Stätte von Königin Lupas legendärer Festung (2 Stunden einplanen für den Rundweg und die Zeit, sich durch das Unterholz zu schlagen). Es gibt noch immer überraschend wenige Cafés oder Geschäfte auf der Strecke, daher sollten Sie vor dem Verlassen von Padrón Ihre Vorräte auffüllen.

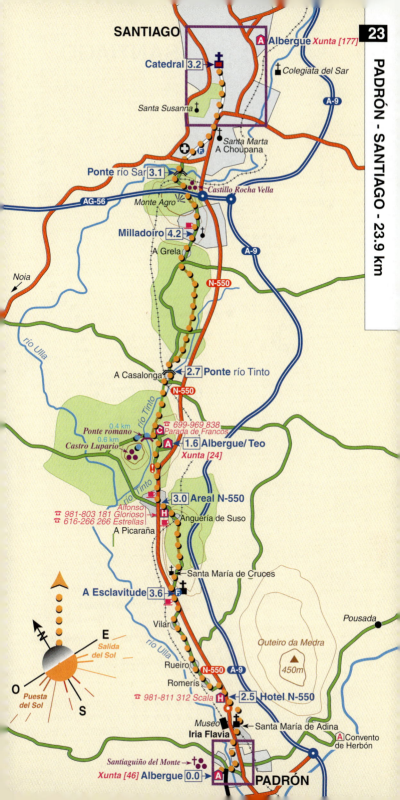

SANTIAGO

Noia

Piscina

Campus Universitario

Tenis

Pontevedra

Av. Burgas

Camino Portugués

Av. Rosalía de Castro

Praza Roxa

Puesta del Sol

Salida del Sol

Argentina

B-Nor

Oficina Xacobeo

Av. Coruña

Sta Rosalio

Pilar

Iberia

Xeneral

Autobus Aeropuerto

Herradura

RENFE

Parlamento

Av. Xoan Carlos

Av. Compostela

SANTA SUSANA (ALAMEDA)

Parque

Poza de Bar

Camino Finist...

Sar Lo...

Rua do Pombal

Alameda

Viloria

Porto Faxeira

Entrecercas

Universal

Praza Galicia

Mapoula

Suso

Avenida

Rua do Horreo

Santo Antonio

Rua Franco

Rua Vilar

Nova

Correos

La Estela

Fonseca

Raxoi

Policia

Hospital

Rua das G...

Hortas

Cruz

BB

Prazo Obradoiro

Museo

Catedral

Casa Deán

Oficina de Peregrino

Rua Vilar

Sta.Catalina

Xelmirez

Quintana

Arte Sacra

San Paio

San Fiz

La Enseñanza

Convento María

*Virxe da Cerca****

Mercado

Prazo Inmaculada

San Martiño

Seminario Mayor

Hostal Reyes Cat... Parado...

San Francisco

San Pico Sacro

Conve... Fran...

C.S.Juan

Estrela

Azabacheria

Costa Ve...

Museo Peregrino

S.Roque

Mou...

Mou...

San Roque

Parque

Seminario Menor

Rua de Trompas

Belvis

Rua de Belvis

Tatona

Fontinas

Virxe da Cerca

Casas Animas

Algalia

Miguel

Giadas

Porta do Camiño

Pantheon Galego

Santo Domingo de Bonval

Igreja San Pedro

Rodas

Museo do Pobo Galego

Parque

RENFE

Camino Francés

Rua San Pedro

Cruceiro

Av. de Lugo

Concheiros

Xunta Galic...

● ● ● ● ● ● Camino Finisterre
● ● ● ● ● ● Camino Francés
● ● ● ● ● ● Camino Portugués

Santiago city: We will each experience different emotions on arrival ranging from euphoria to disappointment but gratitude for our safe arrival is a universally appropriate response. If you are overwhelmed by the crowds consider returning later when you feel more composed and the cathedral is, perhaps, quieter and follow the ancient pilgrim ritual of ascending the stairs behind the altar to 'hug the apostle.' The four squares surrounding the cathedral are: *Praza das Praterías* the traditional entry for pilgrims arriving from Portugal where we also find the pilgrim office that issues the certificate of completion *compostela* – further along Rua Vilar are the 2 main tourist offices. *Praza da Quintana* provides the eastern entrance to the cathedral and the Holy Door *Porta Santa* opened during Holy Years only. *Praza da Inmaculada* the bleak north facing Azabachería façade and, finally, *Praza do Obradoiro* the city's golden square with the cathedral's dramatic west facing façade and *Portico de Gloria,* universal symbols of Santiago.

Ciudad de Santiago: Cada uno experimentará emociones diferentes a la llegada, que pueden abarcar desde la euforia a la decepción, mas la gratitud por haber llegado bien es una respuesta universalmente apropiada. Si te sientes abrumado por las multitudes, valora la posibilidad de volver más tarde, cuando te sientas más sereno y la catedral esté, tal vez, un poco más tranquila. Sigue el ancestral ritual peregrino de subir las escaleras que hay detrás del altar para «abrazar al apóstol». Las cuatro plazas que rodean la catedral son: Praza das Praterías, la entrada tradicional de los peregrinos que vienen desde Portugal, donde también se encuentra la oficina del peregrino, que expide el certificado de haber completado el camino, la compostela. Un poco más allá, en la Rúa Vilar, están las dos oficinas de turismo principales. La Praza da Quintana es la entrada oriental de la catedral, y en ella se encuentra la Porta Santa, abierta tan solo durante los Años Santos. La Praza da Inmaculada, la más sombría, orientada al norte, está ante la fachada de Azabachería y, por último, la Praza do Obradoiro, la plaza dorada de la ciudad, a donde dan la impresionante fachada oeste de la catedral y el Pórtico da Gloria, símbolos universales de Santiago.

Cidade de Santiago: Cada um de nós sentirá emoções diferentes ao chegar, desde euforia a desapontamento, mas gratidão por uma chegada em segurança é uma reacção universalmente adequada. Se as multidões o incomodam, pense em voltar mais tarde, quando se sentir mais sereno, e a catedral, possa estar, talvez, com menos movimento e siga o ritual peregrino antigo de subir as escadas situadas por detrás do altar para "abraçar o apóstolo". As quatro praças em redor da catedral são: *Praza das Praterías*, a entrada tradicional dos peregrinos vindos de Portugal onde encontramos também o posto dos peregrinos que entrega o certificado de completação *Compostela* – mais adiante na Rua Vilar estão os 2 postos principais de turismo. *Praza da Quintana* dá acesso à entrada leste para a catedral e para a *Porta Santa* aberta somente durante Anos Santos. *Praza da Inmaculada* a fachada de Azabachería virada para o tristonho lado norte e, finalmente, *Praça do Obradoiro* a praça dourada da cidade com a dramática fachada oeste da catedral e o *Pórtico de Gloria,* símbolos universais de Santiago.

Die Stadt Santiago: Jeder von uns wird bei der Ankunft unterschiedliche Gefühle haben, von Euphorie bis zu Enttäuschung, aber Dankbarkeit für unsere sichere Ankunft ist eine allgemein angemessene Reaktion. Falls Sie sich von den Menschenmengen überwältigt fühlen, kehren Sie später zurück, wenn Sie gefasster sind und die Kathedrale vielleicht ruhiger ist, und folgen Sie dann dem alten Pilgerritual, die Treppen hinter dem Altar hochzusteigen und 'den Apostel zu umarmen'. Die vier Plätze um die Kathedrale herum sind: *Praza das Praterías* – der traditionelle Eingang für aus Portugal ankommende Pilger, an dem wir auch das Pilgerbüro finden, das die Urkunde über die Beendigung der Wallfahrt – die *compostela* – ausstellt. Weiter entlang der Rua Vilar befinden sich die zwei Haupt-Touristeninformationen. Über die *Praza da Quintana* ist der östliche Eingang zur Kathedrale zu erreichen, die Heilige Tür, *Porta Santa*, wird nur während der Heiligen Jahre geöffnet. *Praza da Inmaculada,* mit der düsteren, nach Norden ausgerichteten Azabachería-Fassade, und schließlich *Praza do Obradoiro,* der goldene Platz der Stadt mit der dramatischen, nach Westen ausgerichteten Kathedral-Fassade und *Portico de Gloria,* allgemeine Symbole von Santiago.

You are encouraged to join your local confraternity, many of whom issue their own 'pilgrim passport.' An official *credencial*, issued by the cathedral authorities in Santiago and readily available within Spain, can be obtained from the Igreja dos Martíres in Lisbon and the cathedral in Porto. A rubber stamp *sello* (Spain) *carimbo* (Portugal) can be obtained from hostels etc along the way and establish your pilgrim progress and status which is essential in order to stay in pilgrim hostels within Spain and to apply for the certificate of completion *compostela* in Santiago. The following pages are provided for personal records.

Te animo a unirte a tu asociación o confraternidad de peregrinos local, muchas de las cuales expiden sus propias credenciales de peregrino. Las autoridades de la catedral de Santiago expiden una credencial disponible en España, que también se puede obtener en la Igreja dos Martires en Lisboa y en la catedral de Oporto. Se puede obtener un sello, carimbo en Portugal, en los albergues a lo largo del camino, lo que establece el progreso y estatus del peregrino, esencial para alojarse en los albergues de peregrinos en España y para solicitar el certificado de haber completado el camino, la Compostela, en Santiago.

Encorajamo-lo a fazer parte da sua associação ou confraternidade peregrina local, muitas delas emitem o seu próprio passaporte ou credencial do peregrino. Uma credencial oficial é passada pelas autoridades em Santiago, na Espanha, assim como na Igreja dos Mártires em Lisboa e na Catedral no Porto. O carimbo, sello en Espanha, pode obter-se nas pousadas, pelo caminho, e mostra o seu progresso e estatuto como peregrino, que é essencial para poder ficar em pousadas para peregrinos em Espanha e para requerer o certificado de completação ou Compostela em Santiago.

Ich empfehle Ihnen, Ihrer Pilgergesellschaft oder -bruderschaft vor Ort beizutreten; viele von ihnen stellen ihren eigenen Pilgerausweis oder credencial aus. Die Behörden der Kathedrale in Santiago stellen ihren eigenen credencial aus, der in Spanien einfach erhältlich ist und den Sie von der Igreja dos Martíres in Lissabon und der Kathedrale in Porto bekommen können. Einen Stempel – sello in Spanien, carimbo in Portugal – können Sie von den Herbergen etc. entlang des Weges bekommen. Damit können Sie den Nachweis für Ihren Fortschritt und Status als Pilger erbringen, was sowohl für die Unterkunft in Pilgerherbergen in Spanien wichtig ist wie auch für die Bewerbung um die Urkunde für die Beendigung des Weges – die Compostela – in Santiago.

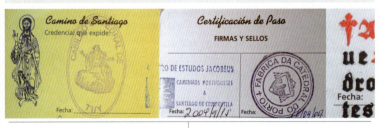

Afterthoughts: The evolution of human consciousness is gathering apace. One manifestation of this is the increasing interest in taking time to go on pilgrimage to reflect on life and its direction. Whilst great care has been taken in gathering information for this guide, it requires feedback from pilgrims who have just walked the route for it to stay fresh and relevant. If you would like to share observations please email your feedback to **jb@caminoguides.com** where updates are posted and can be downloaded gratis from the website **www. caminoguides.com**. If you intend to walk another camino in the future check out alternative routes on the map overleaf. It is not generally known that there are 12 main waymarked routes through Europe, all converging on the fabled city of St. James of the Field of Stars *Santiago de Compostela.*

Reflexiones: La evolución de la conciencia humana es cada vez más acelerada. Una manifestación de ello es el creciente interés por realizar una peregrinación para reflexionar acerca de la vida y la dirección que toma. La información para crear esta guía se ha reunido con gran cuidado, pero para mantenerse al día y que continúe resultando de interés requiere los comentarios de los peregrinos que acaben de realizar el camino. Si deseas compartir tus impresiones, por favor envía un email a **jb@caminoguides.com**. En la página web **www. caminoguides.com** se cuelgan los comentarios y se pueden descarga gratis. Si tienes la intención de recorrer otro camino en el futuro, mira nuestras rutas alternativas en el mapa que encontrarás al dorso. No es muy conocido el hecho de que existan 12 rutas principales marcadas por Europa, que convergen en la mítica ciudad de «Santiago del Campo de Estrellas», Santiago de Compostela.

Reflexões: A evolução da consciência humana está a acelerar. Uma das suas manifestações é o aumento de interesse em arranjar tempo para ir em peregrinação para reflectir na vida e na direcção da mesma. Embora grande cuidado tenha sido tomado ao juntar informação para este guia, ele requer também a experiência dos peregrinos que fizeram a rota recentemente para que a informação se mantenha actual e relevante. Se quiser partilhar observações, envie por correio electrónico, por favor, a sua informação para **jb@caminoguides.com** onde são colocadas actualizações que podem ser baixadas grátis da página da internet **www.caminoguides.com**. Se tenciona percorrer futuramente outro caminho veja as rotas alternativas no mapa da página seguinte. Não é muito conhecido o facto de existirem na Europa 12 rotas principais assinaladas, convergindo todas para a cidade lendária de "S. Tiago do Campo das Estrelas" *Santiago de Compostela.*

Abschlussgedanken: Die Evolution des menschlichen Bewusstseins gewinnt an Momentum. Eine Manifestation dessen ist das zunehmende Interesse, sich die Zeit für eine Pilgerreise zu nehmen, um über das Leben und seine Richtung zu reflektieren. Die Informationen für diesen Reiseführer sind sorgfältigst zusammengetragen worden; trotzdem brauchen wir das Feedback von Pilgern, die die Route gerade gewandert sind, damit er aktuell und relevant bleibt. Wenn Sie Beobachtungen mitteilen möchten, so senden Sie bitte Ihr Feedback an **jb@caminoguides.com**. Aktualisierungen werden in das Internet gestellt und können kostenlos von der Website **www.caminoguides.com** heruntergeladen werden. Wenn Sie beabsichtigen, demnächst einen weiteren Jakobsweg zu wandern, schauen Sie sich die alternativen Routen auf der umseitigen Karte an. Es ist nicht allgemein bekannt, dass es 12 große ausgeschilderte Routen durch ganz Europa gibt, die alle in der sagenhaften Stadt vom 'Heiligen Jakobus des Sternenfelds', *Santiago de Compostela,* zusammenlaufen.

12 Ways of St. James – weeks [•]
12 Caminos de Santiago – semanas [•]
12 Caminhos de Santiago – semanas [•]
12 Jakobswege – Dauer in Wochen [•]

(1) **Camino Francés** 800km [• 5]
St. Jean / Roncesvalles – Santiago

(2) **Chemin de Paris** 1000km [• 6]
Paris – St. Jean via Orléans & Tours
Alt. route from Chartres - also:
Soulac – Tarnos 170km [1 week]

(3) **Chemin de Vézelay** 900km [• 5]
Vezélay – St. Jean via Bazas
Alt. routes via Nevers and Bergerac
Ext. to Namur (B) & Maastricht (NL)

(4) **Chemin de Le Puy** 740km [• 4]
Le Puy-en-Velay – St. Jean
Ext. to Geneva, Konstanz, Prague

(5) **Chemin d'Arles** 750km [• 4]
Arles – Somport Pass
(Ext. to via Francigena, Italy)

Camino Aragonés 160km [• 1]
Somport Pass – Óbanos

(6) **Camino de Levante** 900km [• 5]
Valencia (Alicante) – Zamora
Alt. route via Cuenca – Burgos

Camino de Madrid 320km [2 #]
Madrid – Sahagún

(7) **Camino Mozárabe** 390km [• 2]
Granada – Mérida
(Málaga alternative via Baena)

(8) **Via de la Plata** 1,000km [• 6]
Seville – Santiago

(9) **Camino Portugués** 241km [• 1½]
Porto – Santiago

Camino Portugués 372km [• 2]
Lisboa – Porto

(10) **Camino Finisterre** 87km [• ½]
Santiago – Finisterre

Return via Muxía 114km [• ½]

(11) **Camino Inglés** 110km [• 5]
Ferrol – Santiago

(12) **Camino del Norte** 830km [• 5]
Irún – Santiago via Gijón

Camino Primitivo 320km [• 2]
Oviedo – Lugo – Melide